COMPUTER N.

FOR BEGINNERS

**The Complete Basic Guide to Master Network
Security, Computer Architecture, Internet, Wireless
Technology, and Communications Systems**

David Brown

TABLE OF CONTENTS

INTRODUCTION

I extend my good wishes and thanks to all those who downloaded the Computer Networking for Beginners. This book serves as a comprehensive guide to equip the readers with the knowledge about the Network Security, Computer Architecture, Internet, Wireless Technology, Mobile, LTE and Communications Systems

The chapters presented in this book will be covering the fundamentals of computer networking and its protocols in a well-defined manner. You will find explanations very easy and clear; you will be able to learn the concepts in a very short period of time.

Computer networking without any doubt has been an exceptional invention. Its endless applications have made the spread of knowledge way easier than before for mankind, and have increased the comforts of human life.

The book has been written for beginners in the field of computer networking. All the technical terms are explained in a simplified way which makes any difficult concept easy to understand. Also, to provide the detailed knowledge of the different protocols for effective network communication, topics like TCP/IP have also been discussed.

Since the machine learning is becoming mandatory for the tech industry to become more competent and authentic, it is now necessary for the newcomers to learn computer networking. This book describes the way in which machine learning and computer networking can be integrated to design better and efficient network security hence, it can provide more secure Internet.

We thank you for choosing this book in spite of the fact that there are already many books available on this topic. It was made sure that all the concepts, explanations and information presented in this book will satisfy the reader's need. Please enjoy!

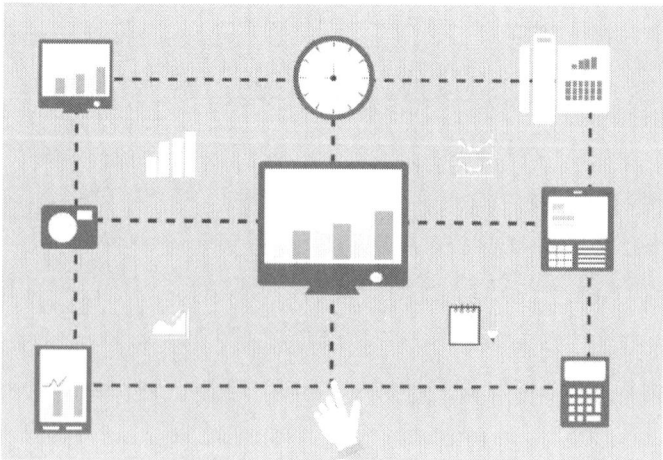

CHAPTER 1
INTRODUCING COMPUTER
NETWORKING

The world of 21st century is a digital world that completely relies on information and computer network. It is very obvious that the relation between information and network is a critical one. The information needs to be transferred quickly from one place to another, and to make it possible a good computer network is necessary. This makes computer network a basis of today's society. Whether it is a transfer of knowledge, or a progress of economy, you have to connect with computer network. Even your social life has been shaped and/or changed by the presence of computer network. Hence, in today's world if you want be ahead of time, you need to remain connected with a network.

Computer networks, Telecommunication networks, and Cable networks are the three basic types of networks. Each of these types serves a special purpose in information processing. Telecommunication networks are used for telephoning, telegraphing, and sending fax. Cable television network is primarily used to bring programs available on our TV screens. However, the most prominent of them all is a computer network which helps people to exchange data between their computers.

The rapid technological advancements have allowed computer network to engulf the other two types. A modern computer network has largely overpowered telecommunication and cable television networks. With a computer network, one can enjoy benefits of telephonic communication, video conferencing, and video streaming. Examples like Skype and Netflix have proven that computer networks are expanding their boundaries and applications and moving out of their intended frame of application. Although one can wonder about the possibility of combining the three types of networks, it is easier said than done.

The first actual computer network was ARPAnet which was designed by Defense Advanced Research Projects Agency (ARPA) in 1969. It is astonishing to realize that the computer networks made all this progress in the last 5 decades only. The fact that the first-gigabit connection has grown magnanimously in such a short span of time seems surreal. The advent of Internet in the 1990s further boosted the development of the computer network and it is now considered a global platform where one can do everything from e-learning to e-business to scientific research. This transformation of computer networks has been inspirational in the truest sense and any decrease in its popularity is nowhere in sight. It can be predicted that computer network and technology will only grow and offer more revolutionary applications. So, let us start by understanding what a computer system is.

We are living in the age of Big Data, where terms like information, communication, and society are used interchangeably. Exchange of information is no more bound by constraints of time and space. And the only reason we have been able to achieve all this is because of computer networks.

Every useful thing comes with its personal set of challenges and the internet is no different. As the demand for more efficient and faster means of data transfer grows, the need to build more robust and complex network systems also increases. In such complex system, one major issue lies with controlling and regulating the routes. Another challenge is to make the network more budget-friendly and accessible. Expert are striving to release the updates into the market at a competitive pace and providing necessary maintenance support to these advanced networks. These challenges can only be addressed by bringing more technically-apt professionals into the pool and train more people to fill the gaps.

Computer these days are just a hand away and have taken over the community. Considering the unstoppable growth of the computer in its various forms, it can be easily stated as "the greatest inventions of all times". Nowadays computers are not only confined to offices, factories or national-international level institutes but these devices can easily be found in your pocket. All your data, files and contact numbers are just a touch away. Tablets, laptops, and smart phones are portable forms of this technology. The huge sized machines were replaced when innovators had hit a novel idea of installing small chips inside of appliances that look nothing like a proper computer but had the potential to grant it a computer control. Working with computer means working with a network and surprisingly we've been introduced to the networked world.

With time, a stand-alone computer, which had a high time once, lost its worth as many other forms of computer emerged. People now prefer connecting to the world in seconds by being a part of a network. Networking assists people to communicate and share their files to someone at the other corner of the world with two or more computers connected. These are usually established within a large scale industry for a private network. The idea of a private network was having hype so the thought of advancing the grounds of networking was put into consideration and gradually, through expansion a private network opened a gate to the Internet; connecting several private networks.

Talking about the internet, the fact cannot be ignored that it grasped a lot of attention in a small period. This cyberspace does not only allow information sharing within an industry but also supports other modes of communication including telephone, fax and letters.

Therefore, the internet met a lot of new modifications with time. It now has the proficiency to integrate with every kind of interfacing medium such as devices, software, hardware, software and transmission protocols making the communication environment much reliable and distinctive.

With the excessive evolution over the internet, the information grid has been expanded. Web, in the information network, is the nerve through which we get access to our desired information across the world. Sharing a personal activity in a group over a social site can minimize the distances between the group members and keep them updated about each other's recent commotions; subscriptions allow every member to be notified about the latest information. These are considered as the real-time examples of web networking. Through blogging, people can share their perspectives and thoughts which can be accessed by everyone subscribed to it.

Definition of Computer Network

It is the connection established between a set of programmable hardware including computers with the particular aim (such as to transfer data or video signals). Various types of data can be transferred through this hardware and hence, it has an extensive range of applications.

The above definition clarifies that Computer network is highly functional for every kind of device and may also incorporate devices other than computers such as smart watch, smart phone, AR devices and others. A computer network is not, in any way, limited to data transfer; rather, it has an extensive list of applications which is expected to extend further in future.

Nowadays, computer networks are not only confined to transmit and receive data but, as the developments expanded the exposure of the networking, it has the potential of being used in various numbers of applications enlarging the application scope.

Computer networks are apparent in personal computers, internet café and offices in the form of a number of PCs apparently independent but connected with one another through devices called routers and switches. Hence, a computer network can be thought of as a system comprised of two or more computers and networking equipment connected through a transmission medium to provide the connection, whether the two end systems are located independently at the two opposite ends of the world or in the same building. A computer system cannot be used for exchange of information and resource sharing unless it is supported by NOS (Network Operating System), NMS (Network Management Software) and a few protocols.

We can simply minimize all the confusion by stating that a connection is established between computers via connection lines or the transmission medium and setting up a computer network application through which every connected end system can access the shared information and resources irrespective of the size of the computer and its location.

The employment of the OS, NMS and protocols allows the sharing of resources such as software, hardware, audio and video files, documents. These resources can be accessed by all. Networking allows users to access the data stored by the server conveniently irrespective of the geographic distance between the user and server.

Data resource sharing is an expansive field including database resource sharing, software resource sharing and others. Software resource sharing is apparent in case of the data being downloaded from the internet. Other example of software resource sharing is the internal network established within an organization to allow all the employees to access the shared tools in the network as per their requirements. Database resource sharing allows the network users to intentionally or unintentionally get interacted with other end systems just like having an account social site or signing up for a cyber gaming websites. Examples also include the e-mails received from the sites like Foxmail.

There are various types of computer networks which may be classified on the basis of various aspects. The network classification is explained subsequently:

Classification of Networks as per Scope:

1. Wide Area Network (WAN)

This network is expanded over a larger geographical area as compared to other networks, connecting cities and countries through a leased telecommunication circuit and linked switches providing access at high speed.

2. Metropolitan Area Network (MAN)

This is relatively smaller than a WAN but it may encompass LANs. MAN is spread enough to interconnect the users within a city covering an estimated area of 5km-50km through Ethernet technology.

3. Local Area Network (LAN)

It has now upgraded itself enough to interconnect to itself, providing connections within smaller regions such as a computer network within a school or institute. These are also noted as "Campus Networks"

4. Personal Area Network (PAN)

As the name explains well, it is established to connect personal devices of an individual at home or work with no wires involved. It can operate within a range of 10m.

Categorized by the Users of the Network

Public Network

A public network refers to an expansive network established and operated by a state or private Telecommunications Company. This network is functional under Telco's regulations and is accessible to the common people, hence the term 'public'. Any member of the general public can pay a specific amount to the company to connect to such a network.

Private Network

A private network is specifically designed and only a defined commercial unit can access it. Anyone who is not a part of the unit would be restricted from using this network. Organizations with confidential data, such as military, banks, railways, and energy companies have their private networks.

Applications of Computer Network in Real World

The evolution of computer networks has certainly transformed the world. However, before delving into the glorious history of computer networks, it is essential to review some applications of this invention.

It is necessary to start the discussion by first addressing the basic questions associated with computer networks: what's their purpose and how can they be used? Asking this a decade ago would have gotten you just one answer: resource sharing. Computer networks were designed to serve just a single major purpose since there existed no internet at that time neither was there any concept of internal network applications within the LAN. However, with the advent of the Internet technology and the advancements in the computer network systems, the demand for a network escalated and this opened doors for a myriad of applications. It has now become such an integral part of our lives that it's hard to imagine a world without a computer network system.

The numerous applications of computer networks can be classified into two major categories: Commercial Application and Personal Application. Both of these categories have been detailed in the following paragraphs of this section.

Commercial Application

A computer network established for business use comprises of the Corporate LAN, the Internet LAN, and the Internet connected to the Corporate LAN which is meant for external users, including subsidiaries, partners, suppliers, etc. Commercial or business applications of computer networks are supremely significant as they provide the foundation for the personal applications. Resource sharing, network communication, data transmission, collaborative work, remote access and management, and e-commerce are some prominent commercial uses of these systems.

1) Resource Sharing

Resource sharing is one of the earliest applications of computer networks. A network firstly helps a business share its physical resources. For instance, people using a single network can all access the same devices like scanners, printers, fax machines, shared data folders, and recorders. Moreover, software, data, and programs are also shared among the users. It is a common practice that several people at a workplace share a single LAN-shared printer connected to a network. Since it won't be practical to invest in a separate printer for each of the employees, companies save big by resource sharing. Nowadays printers using Internet-shared printing are also available in the market.

Resource sharing is not limited to the physical devices. Taking a step further, a corporate LAN allows a company to exchange programs, files, and data. In this age of big data, having a collective access to the saved public documents, database reports, and downloadable software enhances the entire database system of a business. A file server established in the intranet is the home for all data.

The two primary benefits of this technology are that it keeps the shared data protected by providing controlled access and ensures that the data is shared more efficiently. It won't be wrong to assume that devices like floppy disks, USB pen drives, and removable hard drives have been rendered obsolete by LAN sharing.

It is fascinating to know that we can download and upload data, including audios, videos, and multiple files, on the internet with a single click. And, these are just a few examples of resource sharing by a computer network system.

2) Network Communication

Network communication is another prominent application of the network system. Global businesses are using options like remote network interconnection, remote video conferencing, remote training, and remote consultation to enhance communication. A Group Company connects with its Subsidiary company or business partners connect with each other by employing the Remote Network Interconnection. VPN technology is currently used to gain special access to a commercial website. Based on the requirement, access is granted and networks of all units are interlinked. Some advantages of this application include: ease of communication within the network, better security and convenience for e-commerce, and more sophisticated data management.

Commercial sectors, such as million-dollar corporations, manufacturing giants, and reputable healthcare organizations, have incorporated teleconferencing, remote training, and remote consultation in their daily tasks. This is particularly fruitful because it helps them cut meeting and training expenses by eliminating time and space constraints. It improves problem-solving and helps utilize the most proficient resources to take well-informed operational decisions.

3) Data Transmission

Another significant application is transmission of data. Data Transmission entails popular applications like E-mailing, File Transfer Protocol (FTP), Simple File Transfer Protocol Copy Protocol (TFTP / RCP), and uploading and downloading files. The easiest way to understand this is to look at the file transfer option available in applications like WhatsApp and Messenger. Uploading or downloading desired files on websites with dedicated resources and resource libraries is another great example of how computer network is used extensively for data transmission.

4) Collaborative Work

Computer Network systems are largely used for collaborative work and this has largely contributed in making this world a global village. People living in different time zones or companies operating with international clients come together on a single platform through a network. Different systems employed in different parts of the world work collectively to define certain network communication or network application tasks. Switch cluster, various DNS servers in ISP, and DC (domain controller) servers carry out the load balance of the server to make sure that a network user receives a corresponding service.

Employees working in different branches of the same company can also work together on a single project with this technology. Moreover, Wikipedia, the popular content website, is also working on the same idea. Users can collectively add and edit the content to the website, which is then re-edited and checked by internationally licensed personnel.

5) Remote Access and Management

A computer network, comprising of clients and servers, is accessed by users and managed by administrators. This method is called the remote access and management. This also includes VPN solutions for Mobile Internet Support, which allows people working for a company to enter a shared network without having to worry about the time and location. In this way, employees can get their hands on the desired data or upload the files which others may find helpful. Advanced Windows server system functions, such as "remote Web desktop" and "remote assistance", are quite useful when the network engineer is traveling and wish to use or manage a host or server on the company's internal network through the internet. Anyone with the password to the administrator's account can get access to the private servers and make changes to it even from a long distance.

Electronic Commerce

Today, personal websites are developed by nearly every bigger unit. Promotion of their products to the potential customers globally is one of the reasons. Moreover, "e-commerce" is often practiced which means that many entrepreneurs offer facility of online transfer to the customers. Surely, there will many users of Amazon among you; it is a marketplace where different businesses are allowed to sell a variety of their goods like household appliances, books, expensive jewelry, groceries, etc. There are many similar online markets like Flip kart, Alibaba, etc. facilitating the promotion of products on the site. To differentiate such sites from brick-and-mortar stores, they are named "e-commerce".

Home Applications

Initially, the computer network was not considered to be applied commercially; however, the availability of internet and access to internet broadband facilitated computer networks to penetrate into the homes of the ordinary people. Now, our home broadband connections give an easy access to the internet and streaming websites around the world. Friends and strangers from different parts of world are connected within seconds through software of instant messaging like Twitter and Facebook. Moreover, to make people know about our life, state of work, school and our products and services we can create our personal local area networks and websites.

Home application refers to those things that we use or see in our daily lives. This includes WhatsApp, Spotify, Netflix, YouTube, etc. Home applications comprise of everything that we utilize in a routine like gathering awareness, connecting with people, communication, planning holidays, ordering food, etc. First make a list of your favorite websites and search how they work on Google to get a clearer picture of those websites or internet applications.

History of Computer Networking

This section aims at giving an overview of the history of the development of computer and network. In the 1950s, the computers gained popularity and since then the way of using them has altered a lot.

Various generations of changes have been experienced by the development of the computer network. Immense changes have taken place in the connotation of computer network as well as the Computer Network Technology and network applications have become different when comparing first and second generation. Understanding the complete history of the development of computer network will present a better picture of the developmental stages along with helping in differentiating between the significant technologies of today and the obsolete technologies which shouldn't be included in the learning. Definitely, just like there were humans before human societies, there were computers before computer networks. In general, the following stages give a summary of the development of computer network.

(1) First Generation Computer Networks (Terminal-Oriented Computer Networks)

The very first digital computer of the world was developed in 1946. But at that time, the computers were not common as they were quite costly. Very complex methods were used by computers usually, the programs and data were needed to be first printed into paper tapes or cards and then to process them they have to be sent to the Computing Centre. Transceiver was introduced in 1954, it was a terminal employed to transmit data to computers from punched cards over telephone lines in remote computing centers. Teletype also acted as a remote terminal when connected to a computer from then on, it enabled users to introduce their personal programs on a remote teletypewriter and the computers calculated the results in the computing centers which can too be sent to a teletypewriter for printing which is not near. The fundamental prototype of the computer network was this basic transmission system. Definitely, as these are a history now so we do not need to learn about transceiver terminals and the principle of their data transmission.

The Batch Processing systems were introduced to provide more people with the computer facility. The method of loading user programs and data into the tape or tape in advance which is then read by the computer in a particular sequence is known as batch processing, it allows processing the programs and data entered by the user. The computers at that time used to be very expensive and huge to fit in a small office. Consequently, there used to be computer centers where computer management and operations were executed and the user had to use a cassette or tape in advance to load program and data and give it to these centers.

Operating the computers at that time was a complex task and cannot be used by everyone easily. Thus, a special operator was often required to actually operate the program. The processing time of program might exceed and specially when there are so many users, the user program will take longer to run. In this situation, the user can hand over the program to the computer center and leave.

This was the first generation of computer where a computer host was needed to connect computer networks which are computer servers today, surrounded by one or more terminals acting as a computer host performing batch processing and the data processing and storing cannot be performed at the user terminal. As the terminal is incapable to work individually, it does not represent an actual computer network. Hence, it is apparent that the advent of computer networks cannot be attributed to first generation but to the second generation discussed in the following. "Terminal" refers to basic computer composed of computer parts like CRT monitor and keyboard but without CPU or hard disk for data storage or processing, which we now refer to as "thin clients". As the computer was very costly, people usually don't buy complete computer terminal thus they become the clients of computer centers to save the expenditure.

Sabre-i was a conventional application of the computer networks of first generation. It was an aircraft reservation system created in the early 1950s by both American Airlines and IBM and was practically employed in the 1960s. It was a computer surrounded by 2000 terminals around the United States. The responsiveness of the computer system decreases when the load on the computer in the computer center increases and can even result in a server crash.

A single host system cannot be highly relied upon as it halts the entire computer network system when the computer host is halted. The advent of the TSS (Time Sharing System) was experienced by the next batch systems in the 1960s. It was a kind of a system where one computer was used to link multiple terminals that have input and output devices like a keyboard, a monitor, and a typewriter (in the beginning) which means that more than one user can use a single computer at one time. As the computers were very expensive in those days, an average person was unable to afford the cost of a proprietary computer. Nevertheless, the aim of "one person, one machine" was acknowledged by the time-sharing system where a user can be comfortable as "they are the only one to use the computer". This indicates the exclusive feature and significance of time-sharing system.

The convenience to use computers has enhanced a lot since the emergence of time-sharing system specifically in interactive operation which means that the results will be provided to the user after complete processing of the computer as per the instructions of the user. It is a very common feature of the computers today and only time-sharing systems made it possible. After that, computers became increasingly human-friendly and slowly a part of our lives.

The era of computer where users can directly operate them emerged through this specific feature of time-sharing system which made it easier. A communication line was used in a time-sharing system which was interconnected to a computer in the center in a star-shaped structure (*) surrounded by many terminals. The relationship between the network (communication) and the computer began after this time.

(2) Second Generation Computer Networks (Packet Switched Computer Networks)

A study started on linking different computers by the experts to eliminate the loopholes of the first-generation and enhance its convenience and reliability. Find the solution to any problem arising. This was the method how technologies today got enhanced. In August, 1964, Baran introduced the initial concept of "store-and-forward" (which will be introduced while learning about switch technology) in the Rand Corporation's research paper on distributed communications. The new technology was studied by the Advanced Research Projects Agency (ARPA) in the National Physics Laboratory (NPL) in the United Kingdom and in the United States between 1962 and 1966. The concept of "packet" was first developed by David Davis of the British NPL in 1966. The very first packet switching system of the world was introduced in December 1969 based on packet technology ARPANET. This is generally known as the initiator of computer networks.

Telephone lines were the bases of the network (ARPANET) which was developed by the Defense Advanced Research Projects Agency (DARPA). It began with an interconnection of four nodes only – Stanford, UC Santa Barbara, UCLA and the University of Utah but within two years it developed into 15 nodes. The network grew into 60+ nodes and 100+ hosts in the late 1970s, across America and linking various research institutions and universities in both eastern and western USA. Moreover, communication satellites were used to bring computer networks in Hawaii and around Europe in connection.

Towards the second-generation, the end-user is connected with the line and equipment resources in the "communication subnet" as well as rich hardware and software resources of the "resource subnet" in the computer network. The term second-generation computer network is given to this "communication subnet" centered computer network.

(3) Third Generation Computer Networks

(Standardized Computer Networks)

The performance of the computer increased by the 1970s, they became smaller and cheap. Hence, computer use became common for general businesses and it was no more restricted to research institutions. The immense rise of the computer usage for ordinary businesses attracted more and more people to research further on the technology of communication between computers to enhance work efficiency.

It was quite difficult to transfer data from computer to computer before the introduction if the communication. External storage media like floppy disks and tape (pluggable devices for storing computer information) were used in those days to save data. The CD / DVD and USB storage – the electronic storage media of today was initially only disks and floppy disks. These media were then transferred to the main computer for storing data. Nevertheless, to read data from one computer to another in real time has now become easier, thanks to the communication technology between computers (linked via communication lines). Hence, it is a time saver.

The access to the computers also enhanced through the communication between them. People can now use more than one computer for distributed processing and achieve the results together. First, a company used to purchase a single computer for business processing and connects computers of different departments of the company, however, it this trend became obsolete.

Every department has to process its data and send to the main computer through communication line which then processes the data and gives the results. This practiced was followed to process data of different departments.

The development of the computers experienced a revolutionary stage after this. To become more user-friendly became the priority in the development of computer; it aimed at providing architecture system with more flexibility to cater more to the needs of the consumers. Many experiments of computer networks were performed with packet switching technology in the early 1970s and the technology of communication began to be studied immensely between computers from various manufacturers.

The second generation of computer network was enhanced by the "store and forward" mode in its transmission mode yielding better results for the utilization ratio of the costly communication line resources. It is because the communication lines in this "store-and-forward" communication process can be shared for multi-channel communication and not limited to only one channel communication. Nevertheless, the second-generation computer network was yet not very efficient as there was shortage of unified network architecture and protocol standards.

Furthermore, the network systems of various companies can only be used on their personal devices and can't have a connection despite the distribution of the second generation computer networks into communication sub networks and resource sub networks. For instance, System Network Architecture (SNA) was developed by IBM in 1974 to facilitate users with a complete range of communication products which are capable to have interconnection and later in Dec 1975, IBM introduced its personal digital Network Architecture (DNA). Distributed Communication Architecture (DCA) of its own was introduced by UNIVAC in 1976. These were the networks that cannot be connected to any other company, they have a set of rules, and they interconnect network communication products within a certain company and only applicable on equipment built by that company.

There could still be no interconnection of the network between various companies. A fragmented situation can be considered for the network communication market where users have a loss in the direction of investment and is not fairly competitive.

It is apparent that enterprises had a great influence on the development of the first-and-second generation computer network technologies. It is because they develop their technologies which suit their market and needs of their customers, as they say can be in the "hundred schools of thought" of the Times. The benefits gained by the companies is clear through "a hundred schools of thought" but "no rules are difficult to square a circle" in the end. Consequently, the products were not universal that were produced by these companies. Thus, none were superior and the selection of development of the computer network to attain substantive progress became complex.

(4) Fourth Generation Computer Networks
(International Computer Networks)

The technology of the local area network (LAN) became more developed and the technology of optical fiber and high-speed Ethernet emerged. Third generation computer network produced Osi / RM architecture which boosted the development of the internet which is the fourth generation of today. The definition of the fourth generation computer network can be "a system that supports resource sharing and data communication using the network software of communication devices and lines". The Darpa's ARPANET and the protocol standard TCP / IP Protocol Specification actually originated the internet. Following is an overview of the internet history: ARPANET protocol was used in 1985 by the National Science Foundation established NSFNET to support scientific research and education; it was overtaken by NSFnet in 1990 as the basic support of the National Network and penetrated from research institutions and universities into the society as the people greatly embraced this network of E-mail, file download and information transmission; the Internet Society was established in 1992; an online browsing tool called Mosaic was successfully introduced by the National Center for Supercomputing at the University of Illinois in 1993 and it was called Netscape later. The National Information Infrastructure Program was also introduced by Clinton in that year and after that in an information society competition was started by the NSF globally for leadership and supremacy. The funds for the internet by the NSF were halted and it completely commercialized the internet at the same time.

A network which can interconnect various computers emerged in 1980s. Multiple computers can be interconnected by this network may it be small personal computers, mainframes or supercomputers. Windows can be processed in the X Window System generally on UNIX and also in the Microsoft's Windows and Apple's MAC OS X. Through these systems distribution of different programs occurs and they run in different windows and an orderly switching can be carried out. The relationship between people and the web strengthened and people increasingly considered the Web as a convenient place. Users are able to operate multiple programs in this windowing system and can also switch tasks between them. For instance, at a similar time you can create a document on a workstation and switch to the host to run some other programs as well downloading the required data from the database server and connecting with friends through email. We have the facility to surf the Internet for free and get aware of the abundant resources there, thanks to the amalgamation of window system and network.

A "one person, one machine" environment was created

by the companies and universities where they gave individual computer to every employee or researcher with the aim of information processing. Nevertheless, this a very costly environment as well as it gives way to several new problems. This was the reason to coin terms "downsizing" and "multi-vendor" (it means computer hardware and software). The purpose of these slogan "connection" (a link between heterogeneous computers) is a network created on the basis of the combination of products from different hardware and software vendors instead of one vendor (in which only same vendor's products can be used for creating hardware as well as software). Connection of computers from various vendors promotes a low-cost network environment. Today we experience the connection of heterogeneous computers through the communication network technology. Personal computers used to be connected to local area networks in 1990 and often implied Novell NetWare system. Nevertheless, TCP /IP are significant when a connection is needed between all types of computers like UNIX workstations, personal computers, mainframes and minicomputers. In this time, E-mail and World Wide Web (WWW) flourished and facilitated spread of information. This helped the internet to penetrate into households from large companies. To catch up with the innovation, manufacturers struggled to interconnect their products as well as to maintain the compatibility of network technology with the internet technology. Only big businesses are no longer striving for compatibility but also a household or Soho (a mini office or Home Office to do business) are hunting for certain web services and products.

The internet, home page, E-mail, Web, etc. have become very popular these days. The Internet has become a part of our daily lives. To access the internet, people commonly use the personal computer today which initiated as only an individual device. Moreover, with an internet connection people can communicate through their personal computers in real time no matter where they are. The field of communication is greatly affected by the spread and development of the internet. Several technologies that have a different aim are also getting connected to the internet. For instance, was implied as communication base.

The product of the internet technology is the Internet Protocol Network. People get aware through the IP network. An internet connection is now significant to communicate on telephone, television broadcast as well as between computers. Moreover, various devices work after an internet connection. People can now connect to the world using their computer through an internet connection for free. People can do communication, searching and sharing of information, controlling remote devices and viewing new reports by connecting to the internet. Nevertheless, it is very easy. Initially, a computer network aimed to link different computers to create a stronger computing environment, to enhance productivity. This remains the purpose from the generation of batch processing to the generation of computer networks, however, now there is a slight change.

Connecting people is among the major aims of modern computer networks. The internet is used by the people to connect with the world, communicate and exchange ideas. It cannot be considered in the initial stage of computer networks. Many changes have occurred in daily lives of people, scientific research, school education and company development owing to the human-to-human computer network. Many people know how to connect internet. Children today can play games online, communicate with their friends on Whatsapp or watch videos online. Increasing number of adults search and access the information in the internet. The conventional postal mail business faced a great downfall due to the emergence of e-mail (comprising of the exchange of a range of photos and video files), through which people can communicate by using the internet. Buying through the internet changed the style of shopping; it made it easy as well as economical. Passengers do not have to stand in long lines for purchasing of air or train tickets which saves time. Moreover, the using internet for transactions like money transfers or stock trading can save much time in financial side.

(5) Next Generation Computer Network

People might inquire about the current generation of the computer, to which the answer is that these days it is a transitional period between fourth and fifth generations. However, everyone is clueless about the actual state of the next generation especially in the long run. The next generation of computer network (NGN, the Fifth Generation Computer Network) is generally assumed to be a combination of Mobile Communication Network, fixed telephone communication network, the internet, IP network and an optical network. Its framework is integrated and open network that can offer different services along with data, voice and multimedia and it is driven by service, call and carry separate network, service and call control separate and is a combined protocol-based, packet-based network. There is a four layer division in the Ngn with regards to functionality, these layers are: media layer, control layer, network service layer and transmission layer. The primary features of the next-generation computer network include integration of the current (which is the "three networks" namely television network, computer network and telecommunication network, virtualization, the internet of things, cloud computing, HTML5 and various other revolutionary technologies.

The primary new technologies will be "Internet of things"

and "cloud computing" which will completely change the current scenario and applications of computer networks. The IBM mainframe can somehow represent "Cloud Computing" where the management platform and the service will be centralized. Various platforms of software and hardware will be provided by the cloud computing operators along with a range of necessary services and management. The enterprise customers can easily purchase through connecting to the cloud computing platform of the operator present on the internet via a comparatively convenient cloud computing client. It saves the huge investment of enterprise clients in computer network software and hardware platform (like routers, internet switches, firewalls, different server systems, etc.)

The latest technology which is working on further expansion of computer networks is the internet of things (IOT). It implies radio frequency identification (RFID) technology, along with infrared sensors, laser scanners, Global Positioning System, and other information sensing devices, meeting the agreed protocols Connecting items (like electric lights, monitoring facilities, electrical appliances, etc.) that are not attached recently to the computer network and the Internet for exchange of information and communication among items, to attain the intelligent tracking, identification, monitoring, positioning and management of items. This will be a universal internet application as through it we can perform the work on electrical equipment switches, home lights, observing home security monitoring facility.

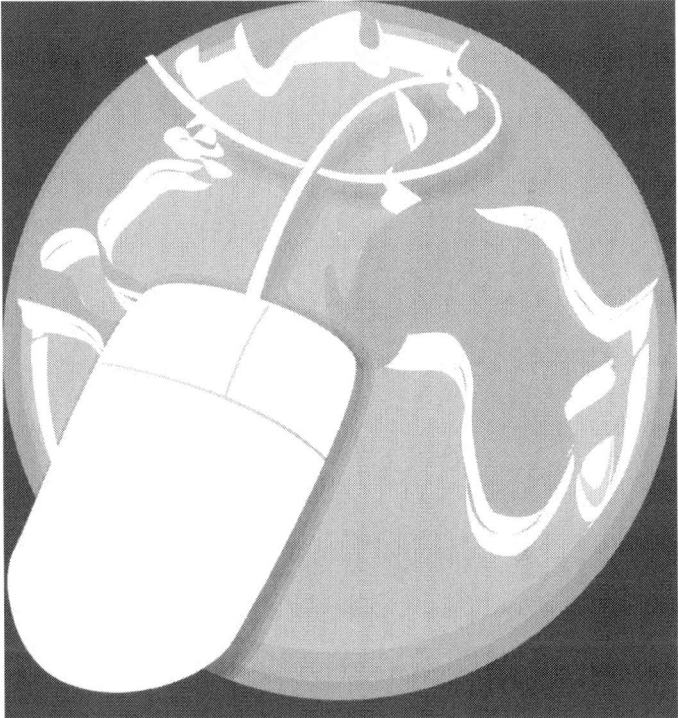

CHAPTER 2

COMPUTER NETWORKING

BASICS

F irstly, the internet will be discussed before coming on the explanation of computer networks. Internet being the biggest network will be explained along with some protocols in which it has communication with the end user to comprehend the Network architecture better.

Why the Internet Has Become a Sensation?

Connectivity and sharing are the major characteristics of the Internet facilitating users with a variety of services.

When users get connected to each other through the internet it is called connectivity regardless of the distance which can for instance be thousands of kilometers. It seems that the terminals have a direct connection with each other due to the ease of exchanging all kind information like data, audio and video which is also not very costly and free in quite a lot of cases. It will be a completely new experience as compared to a conventional telecommunication network.

The world's biggest computer network is the internet. Let's begin with an outline of the internet as well as its primary components to get basic understanding of the computer network.

Different computers are connected in a network whereas different networks are connected in the internet through routers. Mainframe is usually the term given to the computer connected to a network. The size of the internet cannot be estimated as it has overtaken the world as the biggest and fastest developing computer network. 1990s mark the speedy growth of the internet. CERN created the World Wide Web (WWW), which is the European Organization for Nuclear Research. It is now largely implied on the Internet, and is the major stimulator for the rapid growth of the internet as it supports the use of the Internet by non-network Professionals. There is an incredible rise in the number of sites on the World Wide Web. It is very complex to calculate the traffic on the internet however; it increases around 10 percent every month as per the literature of data traffic on the internet.

All the hosts in connection with the internet are at the edge of the internet. End systems is another name of these hosts and "end" indicates "end" of the internet. Every end system has its own distinct function. A normal personal computer (also laptop or tablet), a Smartphone connected to the internet, a big end-system that is the very costly mainframe computer and a small Webcam to observe local weather or traffic and share it in real time on the internet, all are called end system. The end system can be a property of anyone from an ISP (it can have its personal end systems and can also give services to the end system), to a unit (like a government agency, school or an enterprise) or even an individual. The core gives services to the edge which makes various hosts able to have communication and exchanging and sharing of information with each other.

Communication in the Internet

The concepts below should be described first. When it is said that "host A and host B have communication with each other" it refers to "a communication between a program that runs on host A and another program that runs on host B". A "running program" is called a "process", thus "communication happens between a process on host A and another process on host B". Generally, there are two types of communication that happens among end systems at the edge of the network: peer-to-peer mode (P2P) and client-server mode (C / s mode). Following explains these two categories.

Client-Server Approach

This approach to the internet is widespread and conventional. When we are online for sending e-mails or searching for any information on the website, we are in the client-server mode (client/server mode). Upon making a call, the called user gets to know about the call through the ringing of the telephone. Basically, this computer communication is an application process performed in the application layer. Definitely, ringing does not matter for the application process. Nevertheless, communication between two application processes is enabled through client-server approach.

Thus, communication takes place between two application processes that are client and server. A difference between the services and the serviced processes is clear through client-server approach. Server program runs on host B whereas the client program runs on host A. Here it shows that the client is A and server is B. a service request is called by client A and the service is provided by server B to client A.

Following are the primary features:

Service requester becomes the client while service provider becomes the server. The core part of the network extends services to be used by the service requester as well as the service provider. Practically, some primary features are also associated with client and server programs normally.

Client Program:

1. Upon the call by the user to communicate, it starts to run and develops communication (requesting service) to the remote server. Thus, the address of the server program should be in client's knowledge.

2. There is no need of special hardware or complex operating system.

Server Application:

1. Service is provided by this program and the design is as such to deal with requests from various remote or local clients at the same time.

2. As soon as it starts up the system is automatically called and runs continuously, waiting to get communication requests from clients globally. Thus, it is not required by the server program to know the client program address.

3. Usually, advanced operating system and powerful hardware is necessary.

Well, the aforementioned client and server means computer processes (software). The person who uses computer is not called a "client" but a "user". However, "client" often refers to the machine on which the client program runs in various papers of foreign literature (client translated to "client") whereas server is the machine where the server program runs. Thus, context should be referred while classifying whether the client or server indicates software or hardware. When talking about machine in this book, we have used "client (or "client") or "Server" (or server) which refers to a "machine on which client program is running" or "machine on which a server program is running".

Peer to Peer Connections

The number 2 in the peer-to-peer, P2P indicates two in English and it can also be used to abbreviate "to" thus it represents communication between two hosts without differentiating service provider and the service requester. There can be an equal peer-to-peer communication between both hosts because they are running peer-to-peer software (P2P). Each host at this time can download a document that is shared by the other host and is saved on its hard drive. Thus, P2P works in this manner. To have a peer-to-peer communication like between (C and D, E and F and C and F), all the hosts C, D, E and F will run the P2P software. Basically, peer-to-peer connectivity can be categorized as a client-server approach; however, all the hosts act as client and server both. For instance, if the services of D are requested by host C, then the server is D and the client is C. But, C can also act as server if it's providing services to F simultaneously.

A big number of peer users like a million are facilitated to work simultaneously through peer-to-peer connections. A peer to peer connection is best represented by BitTorrent.

Various hardware and software operate simultaneously in their assigned roles to provide speedy services like typing a URL in a browser, screening the contents of a web page. If you carefully read, every individual link becomes easy to comprehend. Nevertheless, if you see from a micro perspective, you will become lost as there are numerous hardware and software working together at each stage. Thus, let's see an overview of this process before further exploring it. For you to not get lost in this journey, the introduction below consists of a road map for discovering.

The Complete Picture of the Web

Let's watch the process of accessing a Web server through browser. There is a sequence of interactions that occur between the Web server and the Browser when a Web server is accessed and a Web page shows up. Below are the main interactions.

(1) Browser: "Please give me the web page data."

(2) Web

(2) Web Server: "Ok will do it"

After the completion of this sequence of interactions, the data is shown by the browser on the screen that is received from a Web server. Although, it's a difficult process when a Web page is displayed, it is very easy to connect the browser with the server. The name of the product and the address of the goods we need are typed and send to a Web server when we are doing shopping in an online mall.

(1) Browser: "please process these order data."

(2) Web

(2) Web Server: "okay, Order Data received.

The Browser and the Web server quite easily interact with each other as compared to the complex system to process an order with the sales system once it is received by the Web server as briefed below.

1. Web server is requested by the browser

2. Web

3. A response is send by the Web server to the browser as per the request.

Hence, it becomes easy to understand the interaction point of Web applications like Web servers and browsers. The interaction is similar to the way humans talk to each other and is not difficult to absorb from this point 1.

A mechanism is required to send requests and get responses between Browser and the Web server to allow the applications to interact. Several computers and devices are in connection with each other in this network. Thus, it is important is this communication process to identify the appropriate communication object for sending and receiving request and response respectively. It should also be taken into account that while delivering; the requests and responses could get corrupt or lost. Thus, a mechanism is required which regardless of the situation, the delivers requests and responses successfully. In other words, a mechanism is required that can deliver the digital information to the desired location as request and response are both 0 and 1 pieces of digital information.

The network control software in the operating system applies this mechanism along with distributing labor between routers, switches and other devices. It mainly aims at distributing digital information into small segments. Containers called "packs" are used to ship it. You must be familiar with the word "Bag" when using a mobile phone but it represents postal and courier services here.

A package can be assumed as a letter or package whereas a post office or a delivery company can be thought of to represent a switch or router. The destination information is on the header of the packet and several switches and router relay to decode it and then deliver it to destination gradually in steps. The mechanism underneath is the same regardless of the size whether it's the internet out there, home or corporate LAN.

A Web is made by these two parts along with Web applications like Web servers and browsers. Hence, these two parts together represents a complete image of the network.

We will learn the working of the browser first. Exploration will begin typing a URL in your browser. Definitely, the transfer of data is not the responsibility of the browser only. This is the job of the mechanism that delivers the digital information to send messages for the browser give data. Specially, the messages are sending to the server through the network control software in the operating system.

The protocol stack (network control software called

Protocol Stack) shows up first. The received messages from the browser are packed by the software and control information is included like the address of the destination. Like in a post office situation where you put the letter in the envelope and the address of the addressee is written on the envelope.

Many other functions are also performed by the software like sending packets again on account of a communication error or managing the rate at which data is sent, maybe it can be assumed as a little secretary who aids in sending letters.

Then, the packet is handed to the network card (the hardware which initiates Ethernet or wireless communications) by the stack. The packet is transformed into an electrical signal by the Network Card and delivered through the wire. The network gets introduced with the packet in this way.

The kind of the internet access determines what will follow. The internet can be accessed by the client computer using a home or corporate LAN or it's personal. Unluckily, all of these situations are not present in our exploration, thus, we can look at the example of the client computer which is in connection with a home or corporate LAN. Then, to access the internet, it is connected to the home (FTTH) and other broadband lines through ADSL and fiber.

In this case, a switch or other device acts as a passage for the packets delivered by a network card to reach a router for accessing the Internet. Internet is at the edge of the router and sending the package to the destination is the responsibility of the network operator similar to that of a postman to deliver letters on the mentioned address once we put it in the mailbox.

The data reaches the inside of the internet from the router implied for accessing the internet. Access network is the gateway to the internet. Generally, the internet is accessed through Isdn, cable television, private lines, telephone lines, light and various other line of communication. Access network refers to a collection of these communication lines. A device named Point of Presence (POP) and a contracted network operator is required to connect the network.

Assume a post office that is very close to your home, it's same as the entity of the access point which is a router built for the operator. An access network is used in the Internet to send the packets to an access point first and then delivered to anywhere in the world same like a post office where letters are collected from different mailboxes first and then sent to the destination. The backbone of the internet is behind the access point.

The backbone network has several operators and many routers. The connection of these routers with each other creates a big network; it finally reaches the designated Web server after passing through a relay of various routers. The fundamental feature is just like that of home and corporate routers and is explained in detail in the main text. It means, that the transmission of packets on the internet follows the same method as the Home, Corporate LAN and this stands to be the primary feature.

Nevertheless, the size of the router is different; it's smaller for home than operators. Huge number of network lines can be connected by a high-speed large router. Numerous routers are at the backbone of the internet and have a complex connection with each other and are a passage for network packets.

Moreover, the connection for every router is different as is their size. Home and corporate LANS usually use Ethernet cables whereas older telephony and the new optical communication technologies are used by the Internet to send network packets as well as Ethernet connections. The technology that is now very popular in the network is discussed in this section and it can be called as a very refined technology being crystallized.

Web server is situated in the Local Area Network where the network packet is finally received after going through the backbone network.

Then, incoming packets meet a check post called a firewall. It is similar to a security guard at the door whose job is to check the bags before letting anyone enter. Next one is the cache server. A web page has a portion which is reusable and the cache server stores this reusable data. It is not important to go through the Web server when you want to read the data which is stored on the cache server. Moreover, distribution of messages is done by the load balancers around various Web servers in huge Web sites and content might be distributed over the internet through some services that cache servers. The Web server receives the network packets after this process.

The data is unpacked as soon as the network packet reaches the Web server and is reinstated in the original request message and then it is received by the Web server program. It is performed in the protocol stack (network control software) in the operating system similar to client. Then, the meaning of the request message is analyzed by the Web server program and a response message is made to load data according to the instructions and then deliver it to the client again. The method of sending the response message to the client is completely opposite of the procedure explained above.

Browser shows on the screen the data it read from the web page after the client receives the response. This is the stage where operations to access the Web server are accomplished and our exploration also ends.

How the Internet is connected?

It is an Access Network AN (Access Network) also called local Access Network or resident Access Network. This computer network is of a special type. An ISP has to be used by the user to access the internet as aforementioned. There are a variety of technologies that can serve to access the internet from home and the Internet connection can also be created through various access network technologies. The access network cannot be classified as the core or periphery of the internet. A network that is shared by a client system with the first router (also called edge router) is an access network. Various access networks originate from local area network under coverage scope. The job of the access network is to give internet connectivity to the user acting as "bridge". Initially, this term access network was not used because telephone lines were used to dial into the internet at cheap prices (sometimes a few thousands or few ten thousands of bits per second).

Basic Components of Computer Network

Hardware equipment and corresponding software system make a complete system of computer network regardless of any aforementioned definition. Network connections and communication equipment, transmission media, network communication software (also network communication protocols) and computer (or a computer terminal having basic computer functions) are the major objects of a computer network.

Hardware systems and software systems are the primary classifications for the components of computer network.

Computer Network Hardware System

The physical support in the computer system that can be seen is called the computer network hardware system which consists following three main parts; transmission media, network equipment and every type of computer equipment.

Computer Equipment

Creating a platform for network communication between the users of multiple computer components is the aim behind developing a computer network. The components include file sharing, data transmission, access, remote control, etc. There is a range of computer devices which are under the network users' use and control like computer servers, computer terminals, PCs, laptop computers, iPad, etc. These computer devices are used to carry out the major applications of the network. Today, there is an overlapping of computer network and telecommunication network. Computer networks and telecommunication terminals are now in connection like data transmission between USB interface and the computer can be carried by the smartphones and also on the remote communication.

A fully functional physical computer (also terminals) is needed in computer network as per the definition. The advent of Network virtualization technology made the computer network a virtual machine like VMWare, VPC, etc. which recreate various individual computer systems in a physical computer developing a virtual computer network. Functions that were once restricted to various physical computer networks can now be carried out on this network.

Network Equipment

Besides computer equipment, network equipment means equipment in a computer network system like bridge, switch, hardware IDS (intrusion detection system), gateway, network card, hardware firewall, router, broadband access server (Bras), hardware IPS (intrusion prevention system), UPS (uninterruptible power supply) and so on, WLAN AP, WLAN Network Card, WLAN switch, WLAN router, etc.

The network topology in the "communication subnet" is built by network equipment and combined with the communication lines ("transmission medium") becomes the structure of the entire computer network. Definitely, network equipment is not required in a simple network which is a computer having two terminals with serial/parallel port cable having a direct connection with the peer-to-peer network. However, as this type of computer network is not of much importance practically, it will not be considered as a computer network.

Transmission Medium

A network line is referred to as the transmission medium, it can be said a network communication "road". Just as to move further we need a road, the network communication will be unaware of the transmit location without these transmission media and cannot transmit. Definitely, transmission medium is categorized as physically tangible or invisible like twisted pair, optical cable (also known as an optical fiber), coaxial cable (which is also used in cable television), etc. For instance, electromagnetic waves are the transmission medium implied in multiple wireless networks. The connection of each node in WCN is identified by Wireless Computer Network (WCN) through electromagnetic wave, obviously, in the twisted pair, coaxial cable, optical cable, and these transmission media.

Computer Network Software System

Computer communication network has computer

hardware system associated as discussed above and application software as well. The computer program installed in the terminal computer for computer network communication or application means the computer network communication and application software. Firstly, a network application platform is present like installed servers and computers along with the computer network communication functions of the operating system. Devices like firewalls, switches and routers can be used to install Operating Systems for computer network communications. Some of its examples are IOS for IOS, Linux, Windows, UNIX, CatOS for Cisco Switch/router/ Firewall and Comware for H3C switch/router/ firewall.

There are network communication protocols too along with the operating system like PPP, Ieee 802 protocol cluster, VLAN, BGP, TCP / IP Protocol Cluster, IPX / SPX, STP, OSPF, RIP, etc. Lastly, it is essential to perform various special network application tool software like our common Qq, Firefox, Sendmail, Outlook, MSN instant messaging software and other email software needed for dial-up PPP, PPTP, L2TP, PPPoE protocol IPSEC and many others for VPN communications.

How the Internet is given to People?

Internet Communications

To make it interesting, let us learn about the construction of the actual network. Usually, Internet access services are utilized through the Internet by individuals at home or at work. Through the Internet, the traffic which is converged to the Wireless LAN router and the nearest switch gets connected again to the "access layer", as previously discussed. However, if the company or network is big or external access is high, it may directly connect to the "Edge Network". The communication with the target address via an "edge network" or "backbone" is probable as well.

Mobile Communications

The phone automatically communicates wirelessly with the nearest base station when it gets switched on. There is a special cell phone base antenna in the base station and the "access layer" of the network is referred to as the base. The base station receives the request when a signal is sent by one cell phone to another, which registers the phone number on the other terminal. The communication connection between the two phones is created when the call is taken by the recipient. The base station that receives the communication requests is in the Control Center ("Edge Network") that is further linked to the backbone of the Interconnection Control Center. The structure of this mobile network is similar to the structure of an Internet access service.

LTE and Voice Call

This has limited data communications. And LTE is referred to as the transition technology from 3G to 4G, a mobile communication standard made by 3GPP, which is an organization consisting of standardization bodies from various countries, that establishes the 3rd Generation Mobile Communication Standard. Achieving up to 300 Mbps down and 75 MBPS UP wireless communications is possible based on the circumstances.

As voice is transmitted as an IP packet, it is required in the LTE standard to employ TCP / IP throughout the network. Now a days, to a large extent, voice communications are digital and utilize TCP / IP Technology. In actual circumstances, nevertheless, simultaneous changing of all the hardware devices of the network is not feasible. For this, the employment of the techniques of CSFB (CSFB) is an option. With this technology, voice calls can be transmitted only over cellular networks. It synchronizes with the original sound process.

CHAPTER 3
NETWORKING IN DETAIL

Initially, the computer network was designed for the reason of linking individual computers to make a strong computing environment and, speaking precisely, for improving productivity. The analysis of the time-period from batch processing to computer networks supports this reason as well. Nevertheless, over time, the technology transitions have taken place.

Among the main functions of the contemporary computer networks, linking people to each other is a major one. Around the globe, individuals can connect, communicate and discuss ideas through the internet, which could not be achieved during the initial phase of the computer networks. With time, individuals have experienced a lot of modifications in their daily life, school education, scientific research and company development, because of this human-to-human computer network.

In this chapter, the computer networking architecture will be explained comprehensively, so that you can easily comprehend the complex process of computer networking. For your easy and good comprehension, the explanation of the topic will be supported with different examples and scenarios.

Protocol

When computer network and information communication are mentioned, a term "protocol" is commonly used. Some examples of widely used representative protocols on the internet are IP, TCP, HTTP, etc. In LAN (local area network), the widely applied protocols are IPX / SPX (NetWare system protocol developed by Novell), etc.

Why Protocols are needed?

When we send an E-mail or browse a home page to generate information, the reconfiguration of computer's network connection and changes in the network settings are to be done. However, during this process, the protocol behind this is unknown to us. We are usually not bothered about protocols and similar aspects, if the network is properly set up and we are smoothly connected to it. The network connection created by the individuals can be easily used by them, if the application can leverage the protocols. At the same time, it may also occur that if an individual is not aware of some protocols, he may not be able to access the Internet frequently and smoothly. Nevertheless, the protocol is a significant factor in the process of communication via the network, and if you understand protocols, this will aid your comprehension of the under-discussion topic as well.

Precisely, an "agreement" that the client computer and the

server computer form during the communication via the network is referred to as the protocol. Because of this "convention" and by using the same protocol, computers, built from a combination of various devices from various vendors, various CPUs and various operating systems, can communicate with each other. In the opposite scenario, communication is not possible if the same protocols are not followed. This can be explained with the example of two individuals who are talking in different languages and hence, are unaware of what the other person is saying. Various types of protocols, having their distinct codes of conduct, are available to be used. For processing and making mutual communication possible, two computers need to support and use the same protocol.

For good comprehension, it is important to understand two fundamental topics before digging deeper into the topic of protocols. Those topics are: the central processing unit and operating system.

CPU

CPU (Central Processing Unit) is often referred to as the "heart" of a computer. All the programs are planned and performed by it. The processing execution and speed of a computer is directly and largely linked to the performance of the CPU. Therefore, an association between the history of the computer and the history of the CPU is commonly made. Currently, individuals widely use CPU Intel Core,

Intel Atom, ARM CORTEX, etc.

Operating System

Os (Operating System) is like a basic software that synchronizes various vital functions, such as the CPU management, memory management, computer peripherals management, program management, etc. Often, the treatment of TCP or IP protocols (explained before) has already been incorporated in certain operating systems. The operating systems widely used these days in personal computers are: are UNIX, Windows, and Mac OS x, Linux, etc.

In a computer, the commands that can be run are dependent on the differing features of the CPU and operating system that are used in it. This indicates that if the programs are designed for some specific CPUs or operating systems, they may not directly run when copied onto the computers having varying types of CPUs or operating systems. The CPU and operating system also affect the storage of data in a computer. Hence, for the communication between the CPU and the operating system of various computers to occur, it is required that IT has a party to support the protocol as well as use it for data reading. This explains why an android application cannot be run in an iPhone.

Furthermore, generally, it is possible for a CPU to run

only a single program at one point in time. For simultaneous running of multiple programs, the operating system indulges in a method referred to as multitasking, in which it adopts the CPU time slice rotation mechanism and shifts between multiple programs and schedule practically.

So What Is An Agreement In Protocol?

Agreements are similar to conversations between individuals. For instance, let us suppose there are three individuals: Sam, Tom and Jerry. Sam knows Chinese, Tom knows English, while Jerry knows both the languages. How would Sam and Tom or Tom and Jerry communicate?

Treat Chinese and English as "agreements" and "Use Chat communication" while considering what is being said as "data."

Presumably, communication between Sam and Tom is not possible unless they both know and talk in the same language. As it is not the case and the agreement (language) used in their communication is not the same, none of them can transmit the data (what is being communicated) to the second individual. Like the gateway in a network environment, an interpreter can simplify the process of communication between the two individuals.

After this, let us discuss about the communication between Sam and Jerry. Through the same "agreement" in Chinese, these two can easily converse and comprehend each other. This is similar to saying that Sam and Jerry follow the same protocol for easy conversation and transmission of the desired data (what needs to be communicated).

Taking this example, it can be said that agreements are similar to the language of ordinary speech. Language is considered a human property by many. However, when computers communicate with each other through the Internet, this communication also makes use of something similar to a human "language". Likewise, there many everyday actions that we do not pay much heed to, but they fall in the category of "agreement".

Protocols in Computers

Humans are blessed with the intelligence to comprehend, analyze and use the knowledge and information they gain in different ways. This indicates that communication among humans does not follow restricted rules. Even if they do have to follow certain rules, their natural adaptability aids them in adhering to those. Nevertheless, this sort of adaptability is not present in the computer communication, as there is still no match between human intelligence and computer intelligence. Therefore, there are set rules, which have to be strictly followed throughout the system, from the physical connection of a computer to the software of an application.

A former agreement sets the basis for true communication. Along with this, the programs to carry out the vital functions of communications should be present and installed in every computer. Continuing with the above-mentioned scenario, if you take a computer in the place of Sam, Tom and Jerry, and the significance of defining protocols as well as adhering to the established protocols while designing software and building computer hardware can be recognized.

Generally, individuals do not have to focus on the pronunciation aspect while speaking; it comes naturally to them. At the same time, even if required for the clarity purposes, adaptability of expressions to other individual's semantics, voice or expression can easily be achieved for better communication. If an individual misses out on some words during the communication, he/she can easily deduce the general meaning of other individual's message in the communication process from the context of the overall conversation. Computers are not able to achieve this. It means that the designing of computer programs and hardware requires attention with respect to the communication process to incorporate exception handling of the various exceptions that might arise. If an issue surfaces during the communication between the computers, the computers need to have the required equipment and programs to handle the exception.

A pre-decided detailed agreement has to be made and adhered to for the computer communication to take place. This is referred to as "agreement" in the protocol.

Packet Switching Protocol

In packet switching method, large data is divided into smaller units, referred to as packets, for transmission. The bag of packets is similar to the bag in the post office. The divisions of data into smaller parts and handing them off to each other are what packet switching involves.

Generally, in the process of mailing a package, a mailing form is filled by the sender, which is then attached with the package to be given to the post office. The information on the form includes the full address of the sender and the recipient. In the same manner, in the computer communications, a source host address and destination host address are provided with every packet that is pushed toward the communication line. The "packet header" includes the address of the sender and receiver as well as the part of the packet number.

In the process of dividing large data into smaller groups, the ordinal number of the group should be included in the package for smooth identification in reference to the association of the parts with the original data. Using this sequence of numbers, the receiver can associate individual packets with the original data.

The information that needs to be written in the start of the message as well as its administration is usually stated in a communication protocol. As specified in the protocol, the computers communicating with each other makes up the starting part of the message and reads the starting part of the content. For proper communication to occur, the sender and receiver of the packet need to have unvarying definition and interpretation of the starting part and the content.

This indicates there needs to be a regulating body of the communication protocol, so that computers from various manufacturers can communicate smoothly. The regulating organization sets standards for communication protocols and international standards. In the following part of this eBook, a detailed explanation of the process of standardization of the protocols will be provided.

The Birth and Standardization of Computer Communications

Systematization and standardization were not the main focus in the early phases of computer communication. The computer manufacturers used to make their individual network products to make computer communication happen, without focusing on systematization, layering and the similar aspects. This changed in 1974, when IBM introduced the SNA that made the IBM's computer communications technology appear as systematic network architecture. After that, the computer manufacturers started releasing their own network architectures, leading to systematization of several protocols. Nevertheless, the compatibility of network architectures and protocols of different manufacturers is an issue. In the presence of two heterogeneous computers physically connected, normal communication is not possible if they have varying network architecture and protocols.

This indicates that the vendor of the computer network products which was selected initially cannot be changed even later on, which may cause problems for the user. In the case of bankruptcy of the chosen vendor or product exceeding the service life, the complete network equipment needs to be changed, which is a hassle in itself. Furthermore, if the physical connection is there, but the employed network products are different, often, even different departments may experience difficulty in communication. Therefore, the users of the computer communication faced problems in terms of limited flexibility and extensibility.

Over time, due to the increased employment of computers in various fields, manufacturers have understood that compatibility needs to be incorporated in their computers. This compatibility enabled the heterogeneous models of the technologies, manufactured by various vendors, to communicate easily. Such changes led to the openness and versatility of the web.

To address and resolve the issues associated with computer communication, ISO (International Organization for Standards) standardized the communication system by setting an International standard, Osi (Open Systems Interconnection reference model). At present, although usage of OSI protocols is limited, however, generally, for the development of network protocols, the OSI reference model, the guideline of Osi Protocol design, is applied.

An additional benefit of the standardization of the protocol is the smoothness of the communication process among the devices following the standard protocol, even if there is a variation in their computer hardware or operating systems. This means that the popularization of computer networks has been facilitated by the standardization of protocols.

There are many companies who have developed several sound technologies, but have not provided proper development specifications publicly, which has led to the limited availability and usage of those technologies. The survival, sustenance and usage of the technologies as well as them becoming industry standards, are directly dependent on the publication of their development specifications by the manufacturing companies.

OSI Reference Model

Prior to the ISO standardized OSI, the OSI reference model was suggested as a communication protocol design index to resolve the issues of network architecture. In this model, the important functions of the communication protocol were broken down into 7 layers. The complicated network protocols get simplified with these layers. Every layer gets a particular service from its lower layer and every layer has to give a particular service to its upper layer. The conventions that administer the interaction between upper and lower layers are referred to as "interfaces". The conventions that administer the interactions between layers are referred to as protocols.

Protocol layering is similar to the modular development in computer software. The OSI reference model is an ideal model, as it proposes to implement all the modules from the first layer to the seventh layer and combine them to enable proper network communication. Through this layering suggested in the model, there is an independent usage of every layer, which limits the effects of any layering alterations on the entire system. Thus, an extensible and flexible system is probable to be created. Further, as the communication functions are divided into layers, assigning separate protocols and certain responsibilities to each layer may require fewer efforts. Therefore, layering has many benefits. However, there are some disadvantages of layering as well, such as over modularity, demanding processing and applying similar processing logic for each module.

Understanding Layering Through Simple Example

Let us take an example of a conversation between Adam and Eve, who are conversing on the telephone (communication device) in English (language protocol). Apparently, the two individuals are involved in a direct conversation in English, however, as a matter of fact; they are speaking in their microphones and listening to the voice of the other through the receiver of their telephone set. If an individual, who is not familiar with a telephone, looks at these two individuals conversing with each other via the telephone, he might think that there is certain networking involved in this act.

At the communications device level, the language protocol of the individual's audio input to the microphone is translated into radio signals, pushed toward the other individual's phones and converted to audio output by the communications equipment layer, which is then transferred to the other individual. This means that the real conversation between Adam and Eve is using an interface between the telephone and the voice converted by the audio.

Usually, individuals consider the phone conversations as direct conversations. However, upon proper reviewing, one can understand that it is actually the telephone that is a mediating device in the communication process and is making the conversation happen. The communication would not have been possible, for example, if the electronic signals from Adam's phone were not changed into sounds, having the same frequency like that of Eve's phone. The same scenario applies in the case of variations in the protocol between Adam's and Eve's phones. The voice might be heard by Eve, but she may not understand if it is Adam. In the case of huge distance in frequencies, she may not even deem that the other person is talking in English.

Suppose, if the communication device layer is altered with the assumption of the same language layer. For instance, replace the telephone with the radio. As radio is being used in the communication equipment layer, the individuals need to know the radio method. However, due to the usage of the English protocol by the language layer, individuals can speak in the same way as they were speaking on the phone.

Now, suppose the communication device layer uses a telephone and the language layer changes to English. Obviously, the language of the user does not cause problems for the telephone. This means it is not much of a different scenario and even now, the individuals can easily make a conversation on call.

In the above stated example, the protocols have been segregated into two layers. In actual packet communication protocols, nevertheless, the layering is not that simple. In the OSI reference model, seven easily comprehendible layers are made for the complex protocol.

OSI Reference Model

The important functions required for communication are properly highlighted in the OSI reference model. While addressing the problems linked with protocol, usually, network engineers prototype the layers of the OSI reference model. Understanding the OSI reference model is the initial step for novices in computer networks, if they want to accomplish in the field.

It is a "model" that provides a general set of definitions of each layer's responsibilities, but it lacks in offering a thorough definition of the protocol and interface. The OSI reference model only provides guidelines for understanding and designing protocols. This indicates that for thorough understanding about the agreement, the specific specifications of each agreement should be examined.

There is a conformance of several communication protocols with the seven layers of the OSI reference model. This means that an overall idea of the position and function of the protocol in the entire communication function can be assessed. Although, for discerning the protocol, a thorough reading of the specification is required, the corresponding OSI model layers can provide the general purpose of the protocol. This is the main reason why OSI model is considered an initial learning concept prior to understanding each protocol.

In the OSI (Reference Model), the communication functions are segregated into seven layers. The standards linked with the protocol and interface of each layer are stated by the OSI Protocol in the OSI Reference Model. Products that adhere to the OSI Protocol are referred to as OSI products and the communications they follow are referred to as OSI Communications. "OSI reference model" should not be misunderstood with "OSI protocol", as they both have distinct meanings.

The OSI layers include: presentation layer, application layer, session layer, transport layer, Network layer, Data link layer, and physical layer. These layers have been discussed below.

Application Layer

This layer offers services to the application and mentions the particulars of communication in the application, such as file transfer, email, remote login (virtual terminal) and other protocols.

Presentation Layer

The information processed by the application is converted by this layer into an appropriate format for network transmission or the data from the next layer is converted into a format that can be dealt with by the upper layer. This indicates that the layer chiefly handles the data format conversion. To be more precise, the data can be formatted by the device into the network standard transmission format. There may be a variation in the interpretation of the same bit stream by various devices, which means that the chief role of this layer is increasing their consistency.

Session Layer

This handles the creation and disconnection of the communication links (logical path of data flow) and data transfer related tubes, like data partitioning manager.

Transport Layer

This layer serves the purpose of a dependable transmitter. Processing is not only carried out on the router, but also on both sides of the communication.

Network Layer

Through this layer, the data reaches the destination address, which may be a single address, connected to multiple networks through a router. This is why the network layer chiefly handles the addressing and routing.

Data Link Layer

The physical level of interconnection, communication between the nodes is handled by this layer. For instance, in the communication between two nodes connected to one Ethernet network, the 0, 1 sequence is divided into meaningful data frames and transmitted to the opposite end (generation and reception of data frames).

Physical Layer

This layer deals with the 0, 1-bit current (0, 1 sequence) and voltage levels, light flash between the exchange.

This short discussion of the reference model and the jargons used in it might have puzzled you. Therefore, for your better comprehension of the communication between the OSI layers, we will present a small example here.

How Do You Modularize Communications in the 7-layer OSI MODEL?

Data is sequentially transmitted by the sender from Layer 7, Layer 6 to Layer 1, whereas data is transferred from Layer 1, Layer 2 to Layer 7 towards each upper layer. The data from the preceding layer can be processed at each layer using the "first" information that is needed by the existing hierarchical protocol. The end of the data is then obtained from the "first" and "content" of the separation, after which it is forwarded to the subsequent layer, after which the end of the data is transmitted back to the initial state.

Handling Above Session Level

If Sam wants to wish Estella "good morning" through email, what would the web actually do? We will perform an analysis from the top to bottom to understand what actually happens in this process.

Application Layer

A new email message is written by User Sam on the host computer (typically in a browser), the recipient is specified as Estella and the message "good morning" is entered. The software used to send and receive emails can essentially be differentiated into two functional categories, where one is communication-related and the other is not. For instance, the non-communication-related function is when Sam writes "good morning" on the keyboard, while the communication-related function is when the message is sent by Sam to Estella. Therefore, the application layer equals to "writing the contents of the e-mail and then sending it to the target audience".

The processing of the application layer protocol starts from the point the user enters the message he wants to send and presses the "send" button. A header (label) is assigned by the protocol to the front end of the data that is to be transferred. In the first part, the message is recognized as "Good Morning" and the recipient as "Estella". This data with the message entered is dispatched to host Estella, after which the mail-receiving software on the host receives the content through the "mail-receiving" function. Following the application on the host, the data sent by host Sam is received by Estella and analysis of the data header and data body is carried out. The data will be then be saved onto a hard drive or some other non-volatile random-access memory, a storage device where it is not possible to lose data even during a power outage. If the mailbox space of the recipient Estella is full and is unable to receive new messages, the sender receives an error. These kinds of exceptions also face problems during their handling and have to be solved using the application layer.

Presentation Layer

"Presentation" in the presentation layer refers to a representation and demonstration. Therefore, the focus is on robust presentations of data (most commonly, the manner in which data is assigned by the computer in memory differently, usually, large and small entities). Furthermore, when different software applications are used, there will be performance of distinct kinds of data. For instance, files are generated by a few word processors that only a particular version of the software offered by the word processor machine can open and read.

So what should you do if you face this kind of issue in your email? If the same mail client software is used by both Sam and Estella, then they may not face any issues in sending and receiving emails. However, this is not likely to happen in reality. It is very inconvenient to get all users to use the same client software in a cookie-cutter manner (in the present times, there are other devices apart from PCs that are also connected to the Internet, like smartphones). It is becoming increasingly important to become capable of reading communications shared between one another.

This issue can be solved in various ways. The first is to use the presentation layer to transform data from "A computer-specific data format" to a "standard network data format" before it is dispatched. Once the data is received, it is restored by the receiving host in the network standard format into the "computer-specific data format", after which it is appropriately processed.

Data was transformed in the preceding example to a shared standard format prior to being processed, which creates consistency of data among the heterogeneous models. This is what the purpose of the presentation layer is. That is, it is a layer that changes the "uniform network data format" and the "data format specific to a computer or a part of software".

In this example, the message "Good Morning" is transformed to "unified network data format", corresponding to its encoding format, even if it is a simple stream of text that can be encoded in different complex formats. For example, consider Japanese, such as EUC-JP, Shift, ISO-2022-JP, UTF-8, UTF-16, as well as various other encoding formats. If you are unable to encode it in a particular format, then at the receiving end, the recipient of mail may also be garbled (in actual life, the situation when the receipt and delivery of mail becomes garbled is not uncommon. This typically happens when the presentation layer does not operate in the desired encoding format, or the encoding format is not set accurately).

To determine the encoding format, the header information will be attached by the presentation layer, and this information will transmit the actual data that has been transferred to the subsequent layer for processing.

Session Layer

We should now examine how to have efficient interactions with data between the session layers of the hosts on the two sides of data transmission.

For example, consider a situation where five new e-mails have been prepared by Sam to dispatch to user Estella. It is possible to send these five messages in any order. For instance, a connection can be established (a communication connection), which is disconnected every time a message has been sent. It is also possible to send 5 emails in a sequence after a connection has been established. Five connections can also be established at the same time, and five emails can be sent to the recipient at the same time. The session layer is mainly responsible for determining the connection method that is most appropriate.

A header or label is attached by the session layer (similar to the application or presentation layer) to the front side of the data it receives before it is sent to the subsequent layer. Information is present in these headers or tags regarding the order followed during transmittal of data.

Handling Below Transport Layer

Examples have been used till now to explain how the overall process of data written over the application layer is formatted and coded by the presentation layer and is then dispatched by the session layer tag. Nonetheless, it is only decided by the session layer when a connection should be established, when data should be sent, etc., and plays no part in when data is actually transferred. It signifies the "Unsung Heroes" beneath the session layer that is actually responsible for transferring particular data across the network.

Transport Layer

It is made certain by the Host that there is communication with host Estella and data can be dispatched readily. This process is known as "making connections", where the e-mail dispatched by host Sam is received by host Estella, and the final data is received by the Mail Handler of host Estella. Furthermore, the connection should be disconnected after communication transmission is complete.

As mentioned earlier, processing should not be connected or disconnected (it should be remembered that the session layer decides when connection should be established and disconnected, whereas the actual connection and disconnection processing is carried out by the transport layer). The transport layer is mainly responsible for generating a logical communication among the two hosts. Furthermore, the arrival of the transmitted data at the destination address between computers at the two ends of the communication is validated by the transport layer, which then transmits the data again if it has not reached yet.

For instance, a "Good Morning" message is sent by a host to Estella. The data may become compromised at this point for some reason, or because of a certain network exception that is part of the data going towards the destination address. If Host Estella does not receive the complete message, missing out on the "morning" part, then it will be informed that it has not received the "morning" part of the data. In addition, Sam will also be informed about the incomplete message sent, and will resend the data to host Estella, and will be asked to verify again if the complete message was received by the other party.

This is like people asking others what they just said in routine conversations. This shows that the fundamental principles of computer communication protocols are closely related to our everyday life.

Therefore, a critical role of the transmission layer is to make sure that data transmission is reliable. Reliability can be ensured by attaching a header to the data that is to be transferred at this layer to determine the hierarchical data. Practically, however, the network layer performs the tasks of transmitting data to the other party.

Network Layer

The network layer transmits data from the sender to the recipient in a network-to-network connected setting. Though there are several data links among the two end hosts, the network layer offers the ability to transfer data from host Sam to recipient Estella.

When data is actually being dispatched, an important element is the Destination Address that is used for communication. The network indicated the unique ordinal number. Consider this as a phone number that is used in our routine lives. After identifying the destination address, the computer used to dispatch the data to the destination address can be determined from several computers. On the basis of this address, there is dispatching and process of packets at the network layer. The address and network layer packet sending processing can be used to dispatch data to any interconnecting device across the globe. The data and address information acquired from the upper layer is also sent by the network layer to the data link layer beneath for subsequent processing.

Relationship between Transport and Network Layer

Under the various network configurations, at times the network layer is unable to guarantee data accessibility. For instance, in an IP protocol equal to the TCP/IP Network Layer, it is not guaranteed that data will be sent to the recipient. Hence, there will be a significant increase in data loss, risk of confusion and other issues during the data transmission process. In this kind of network layer, in the absence of no transmission requirements, it may be the responsibility of the transport layer to offer "appropriate transmission data handling". There is collaboration between the network layer and the transport layer in TCP/IP to make sure that there is dependable transmission of packets worldwide.

When the role and responsibility of every layer is clear, then the specification and implementation (software coding particular protocols to enable them to work on a computer) of these protocols becomes easier

Data Link Layer, Physical Layer

Physical transmission media is used to achieve transmission communication. The data link layer is where data is processed between the devices connected through a transmission medium. Within the physical layer, there is conversion of 0 and 1 of the data into voltage and pulse light for being transferred to the physical transmission medium, whereas connected devices directly use the address for transmission. This address is referred to as a Mac (Media Access Control) address, or a physical or hardware address. The purpose of using the MAC address is to determine devices linked to the same transmission medium. Hence, in this hierarchy, the initial part including the Mac address information is connected to the data dispatched from the network layer to the network.

Data is sent by the network layer and the data link layer to the receiver on the basis of the destination address; however, it is the responsibility of the network layer to transfer the whole data to the ultimate destination address, whereas only the data within a segment is dispatched by the data link layer.

Processing of Host Estella Terminal

The way processing is carried out on host Estella is contradictory to that of host Sam. The processing commences from the physical layer and the data received is dispatched to the preceding layer for processing. Therefore, the mail client software can be viewed by user Estella where the mail sent by user Sam is received. User Estella is now able to read the content received as "good morning". The functions of a communication network can be considered by the reader in layers. The protocol on every layer defines the format of the data header in that layer and the order in which processing of the header and the data takes place.

Classification of Transport Modes

For several classifications, the basis of network and communication can be its data transmission techniques. These can be classified in different ways, some of which are discussed subsequently.

Connectable Oriented vs. Connectionless Oriented

Data can be sent over the network through two techniques: connectionless-oriented, such as Ethernet, IP, UDP, etc., and connection-oriented, such as frame relay, TCP, ATM, etc.

Oriented Connected Type

In connected-oriented type of data transmission, data does not have to be transmitted in groups at the sending end. It can be seen that TCP send data in packets in a connection-oriented manner. Circuit switching is also a connection-oriented form of data transmission, but it does not send data in packets. In this type of data transmission, there needs to be a communication line between the transceiver hosts (connection may be defined in different ways in different layered protocols. In the data link, connection signifies the connection of the physical, communication line. It is the responsibility of the transport layer to generate and handle logical connections).

Establishment of connection is similar to a phone call being made by a person. Once the phone number has been typed and dialed, an actual call is made when the other side picks up the call. Once the call is over, ending the call is similar to cutting off the power. Hence, the connection is established and disconnected prior to and following the communication transmission in a connection-oriented mode. When there is no communication with the other party, sending unnecessary data can be prevented.

Connectionless Oriented

In connectionless-oriented types of transmission, connection does not have to be established and disconnected. Data can be sent by the sender at any time (quite often, packet switching is used for unlinked kinds, where data can be inferred as packet data). On the other hand, it is not known to the receiver where and when it is going to obtain the data. Hence, the receiver in connectionless-oriented contexts has to confirm that data has been received.

It is similar to how people visit the post office to send a package. The postal clerk does not have to confirm if the recipient's address is correct or that the recipient will receive the mail. The sender only needs to have a mailing address to send a parcel. Connectionless communication is different from telephone communication in that it does not need processing, like making a call or ending the call. Rather, the sender has the freedom to send the data it wants to.

Hence, the existence of the receiving end does not have to be confirmed in the connectionless-oriented communication. Data can be sent by the sender even when the received is non-existent or unable to receive it.

Connection-Oriented and Connectionless-Oriented

In human society, the term "connection" refers to "network". Here, it signifies an acquaintance or an association among people. On the other hand, connectionless refers to a lack of relationship among people.

The phrase "where to get the ball!" is commonly used in baseball and golf. This is characteristic of a sender-side processing in connectionless communication. Connectionless-oriented communication may be considered as being somewhat unreliable by certain readers. However, for certain specialized equipment, it is a highly effective technique. It eliminates certain complex procedures, making the process simple. It becomes easier to generate certain low-cost products and decrease the processing burden.

Circuit Switching and Packet Switching

Currently, there are two types of network communication techniques – circuit switching and packet switching. The history of circuit switching technology is quite extensive, and it was used to a large extent in the telephone networks in the past. A comparatively newer form of communication is packet switching technology, which started being acknowledged from the 1960s onwards. The focus of this book is on presenting the TCP/IP that makes use of packet switching technology.

It is the switch in circuit switching that is chiefly responsible for data transfer process. The computer is initially connected to the switch, and various communication lines are used to continue the connection between the switches. Hence, when data is being transmitted between computers, a communication switch between the switch and the target host has to be set up. Connecting circuits is referred to as establishing connections. Once connection has been established, the circuit can be used by the user till the connection is disconnected.

When the purpose of using a circuit is only to establish communication lines between two computers, it indicates that communication between just these two computers is required; hence, the two computers can form exclusive lines of data transmission. However, an issue arises when several computers are connected to a circuit and require data transfer between one another. As one computer has special access to the whole circuit when sending and retrieving information, other computers need to wait till data processing by the computer has ended, before they can use the circuit. During this process, the start and end of data transmission of a computer cannot be predicted by anyone. When the number of concurrent users is more than the number of lines of communication among the switches, it is not possible to have any form of communication.

A new technique was formulated by people to cater to this issue. The computer connected to the communication circuit would divide the data to be sent into several packets in a particular order and then send the data separately. This is known as packet switching. Data is subdivided with packet switching so that it becomes possible for all computers to send and receive data simultaneously, which enhances the use of communication lines. The addresses of the sender and receiver are written at the start of each packet; hence, when if multiple users are being simultaneously served by the same lines, it is still possible to clearly distinguish the destination where each packet is to be transmitted, and the computer with which it is having communication.

A communication line is connected through a packet switch (router) in packet switching. In this process, the sending computer transfers the packet data to the router that receives this packet data, caches it to its buffer and then dispatches it to its target computer. Hence, another name that is given to packet switching is cumulative switching.

After data is received by the router, it is cached into a queue and is sent out turn by turn in a first-in, first-out order (at times, priority is given to data that has a more definite destination address).

Normally, in packet switching, there is a single communication line between computer and router and between router and router. Therefore, this line is a shared line in reality. There is uniform speed of transmission between computers in circuit switching. However, the speed of communication lines may not be the same in packet switching. The time taken for the data to get to its destination may be different, based on the network congestion. Furthermore, when the router's buffer is full or overflowing, the packet data may also get lost and not be received at the receiving end.

Classification By Number of Receivers

The communication in network communication may also be categorized on the basis of the number of target address and its ensuing behavior, for example broadcast, multicast, etc.

UNICAST

"Uni" literally means "1", while "cast" refers to "cast". Therefore, unicast means a one-on-one communication. The landline telephone was one of the foremost examples of unicast communication.

Broadcast

Broadcast literally means to play. It refers to the dispatching of a message from one host to all the hosts that it is connected to.

The television broadcast is a classic example of broadcast communication, where the television signals are sent to non-specified multiple receives at the same time. Furthermore, it is known that television signals usually have their personal frequency bands and can only be received within the acceptance range of the parallel frequency band. In a same way, computers that broadcast communications also have their broadcast range, and only a computer that is within this is range is able to get the broadcast message. This range is referred to as the broadcast domain.

Multicast

Similar to broadcasting, in multicasting, messages are sent to multiple receiving hosts. However, it is different from the former in that there needs to be a particular set of hosts that are qualified as receivers. Video conferencing is the best example of multicasting. This is a kind of remote conferencing in which individuals from different locations are involved. It is not possible to broadcast video conferencing as it would not be possible to know where every recipient was.

Anycast

A form of communication where a single host is chosen as the receiver is known as anycast. This process is similar to multicast as it targets a particular set of hosts; however, it behaves in a different way. The host is chosen in the anycast communication approach from a target host group that best fulfills the network conditions for dispatching the message. Usually, a unicast signal will be returned by the specific host chosen, and the sender host will communicate with that host only.

In real networks, anycast applications have DNS root domain name resolution servers.

Address

The sender and the receiver in communication transmission can be considered as the communication subjects. All of these can be recognized through a message known as "address". For example, when a telephone is used for communication, the telephone number is equal to an "address". When communication is carried out through a letter, the "address" is recipient's address and name.

It is easier to comprehend the actual "address"; however, in computer communications, identifying this address is more complicated. In real network communication, every layer of the protocol used by the address is different. For instance, in TCP/IP communications, IP address, MAC address, port number, etc. are the address identifiers. An e-mail address can be used in the application layer as the address of the network communication.

The Uniqueness of Addresses

Address can play a part in communication by first identifying the actual body of the communication. A principal object should clearly be denoted by an address. It is not permissible for a communication subject having two identical addresses to be present in the same communication network. This refers to the uniqueness of the address.

A question may come to your mind now. It was explained previously that a communication subject having two similar addresses cannot exist in the same communication network. This can be easily understood in the case of UNICAST communications as there is a single host at the two ends of the communication. However, how can this is pertinent to broadcast and multicast communication? There is a logical reason behind this statement. There may be multiple receiving devices in these communications. This is why a unique address is allocated to a group of communications that include multiple devices so as to prevent obscurity and receive communication unambiguously.

Address Hierarchy

When the overall number of addresses are not too many, a unique address helps in locating the main communication. Nonetheless, where the overall numbers of addresses are quite high, a vital issue will be to effectively determine the target address of communication. This is why it has been determined that the address requirements should be hierarchical and also unique. The address hierarchy has been a part of the telephonic and mail communication process for a very long time. For instance, a country area code and a domestic area code are included in a telephone number, and the postal address includes the country name, province city and district. It becomes easier to locate an address because of this hierarchical classification.

Uniqueness is exhibited by Mac and IP address in recognizing a communication body, but hierarchical classification is used in IP address.

The device's manufacturer for every NIC (Network Interface Card), also called a Network Card, define the

Mac addresses. These cards are used by computers to gain connection to the Internet. The uniqueness of the MAC address can be determined by manufacturer's identification number, manufacturer's internal product number as well as the generic product number. Nonetheless, it cannot be identified which network cards are from which vendor and used in which area. Though some degree of information like manufacturer identification number, general number and product number is provided by the MAC address, it does not help in finding the address. Hence, it cannot be considered as a hierarchical address. Hence, though the MAC address is quite responsible for the ultimate communication address, when the actual addressing process is being carried out, the IP address is required.

So how is layering accomplished by the IP address? An IP address includes a network number and a host number. If the main communication IP address is not the same, and if the host number is also distinct, the network number is the same and they belong to the same network segment. Generally, the hosts of the same network segment are also part of the same group or department. In contrast, hosts that have the same network number are centralized within the organization, provider kind and geographic distribution, because of which IP addressing can be carried out easily. This shows the hierarchical nature of IP addresses.

Every node in network transmission will determine which network card should dispatch the packet corresponding to the address information provided in the packet data. For this, each address presents a list of outgoing interfaces. Here, MAC addressing is identical to IP addressing. However, the referencing table in MAC addressing in known as the address forwarding table. The reference in IP address is referred to as the routing control table (presently, the forwarding table and the routing control table cannot be established manually on every node within the network, but are usually automatically generated by the nodes). There is also automatic generation of address forwarding tables on the basis of self-study. In addition, the routing protocol is followed to automatically create the routing control table. It is in the Mac address forwarding table that the actual MAC address is recorded, whereas the IP address that is noted in the routing table signifies the centralized network number.

Network Components

Several cables and network equipment are needed to establish a network environment. In this book, just the hardware that creates a connection between computers is explained.

Communication Media and Data Links

Computer networks signify the computer and computer connected and includes network. It should be determined how connections between computers are established in the actual world?

Cables are used to connect computers to one another. There are several kinds of cables, such as fiber optic cable, twisted pair, serial cable, coaxial cable, etc. A protocol and its network for creating communication between devices that are directly connected are based on data links (Datalink). There are several transmission medium corresponding in this regard. Various kinds of cables are used, and it is possible to differentiate the medium itself into microwaves, radio waves and other kinds of electromagnetic waves.

Transmission Rate and Throughput

Transmission rate refers to the physical speed at which there is data flow among two devices in the data transmission process. The unit BPS (Bits per Second) is used to represent the transmission rate. In strict terms, there is constant flow rate of signals in different transmission media. Hence, if the data link transmission is different, no situation will arise where the transmission speed is slow or fast (as the transmission speed for light and current is the same). A transmission rate that is high does not suggest that there is rapid per unit flow of data; rather it signifies the amount of data that is transferred per unit time.

With respect to road traffic in our lives, low-speed data links signify too few lanes to allow a large number of cars to pass through at the same time. On the other hand, a high-speed data link is a road that has multiple lanes that permits a larger number of vehicles to pass through at the same time. The transmission speed is also referred to as Bandwidth. When the bandwidth is higher, the network capacity is also larger.

Furthermore, throughput refers to the actual rate of transfer between hosts, having the same units as the bandwidth (Bits per Second). Throughput is not only used to measure the bandwidth, but also determines the CPU capacity of the host, network congestion and the number of data fields in the message (excluding the header, and including just the data fields).

Connection between Network Devices

Interconnectivity among network devices should follow some form of "law" of regulations and industry standards. This is an important step in establishing an online environment. If a vendor employs its own transport medium and protocol when creating different network devices, then it will not be possible for those devices to connect to the devices or networks of other vendors. In this regard, a unified agreement and specifications has been created by people. Relevant network equipment should be created by every manufacturer that strictly conforms to the requirements; if this is not the case, then its products will be incompatible with other network equipment, or face the risk of failure.

Nonetheless, norm-setting is frequently a long-term process, and in this process of technological transition, certain "compatibility" issues are likely to surface. This is particularly true in the initial days of the new technologies, like ATM, Wireless LAN and Ethernet. Issues are frequently faced when there is connection between the network devices from distinct vendors. There have been certain improvements over time; however, it is still not fully compatible.

Hence, when the actual network is being constructed, it is not only important to give consideration to the particular parameters of every product; rather, it is also important to comprehend their compatibility. In addition, greater degree of attention should also be given to the precise long-term use of these products. Performance indicators for good technology (also referred to as "mature technology") indicate the market and users who collect a significant extent of practical experience of the technology over a particular time period. There can be serious implications of using a new product without having performed adequate research, because of which it does not work properly.

Network Card

A network card (called the network interface card (NIC)) should be used by any computer linked to the network. The NIC is an integrated device through which the LAN functions can be connected. At times, it is integrated into the motherboard of the computer, or it may be separately inserted into an extension slot. Often, the Network Information Center (Network Information Center) is often referred to as network card, network adapter, or LAN card.

In the recent times, the parameter "built-in LAN port" has been included in various product catalogs. A greater number of computers have the factory settings with Ethernet (Ethernet) 1000BASE-T or 100BASE-TX port (computer and external connection interface called computer port). A computer without a NIC configured should have at least a single external socket to plug in the NIC if it wishes to get connected to the Ethernet. By the PC Card standard PCMCIA (Personal Computer Memory Card International Association) has unified specifications, or a CardBus compressed flash memory and USB plug a piece that is connected afterwards.

Repeaters

A device that expands the network at the physical level, layer 1 of the OSI model is known as Repeater. Adjustments are made to the electrical or optical signals from the cable, and these are amplified by the waveform of the repeater, and then transferred to another cable.

Generally, connections are made between two ends of the repeater and the same communication platform; however, the transfer between distinct media can also be accomplished using certain repeaters. For instance, adjustments can be made to the signals among the coaxial cable and the optical cable. However, here it is the responsibility of the repeater to replace the signal among the 0 and 1-bit streams, and not to identify if there is error in the data. In addition, it is only supposed to change the electrical signals into optical signals. Hence, it cannot be transmitted between media having distinct transmissions speeds (it is not possible to connect one 100 Mbps Ethernet and another 10 Mbps Ethernet with a repeater. To connect two networks of distinct speeds, devices like bridges or routers are needed).

The length covered by network extensions through repeaters is not infinite. For instance, it is possible to connect a 10 Mbps Ethernet in segments with a maximum of four repeaters, whereas an Ethernet of 100 Mbps can be connected using a maximum of two repeaters.

Multiple port services can be offered by a few repeaters,

and this kind of repeater is known as a relay hub or simply hub. Hence, it may also be considered as a Multi-Port Repeater, where every port may be a repeater.

Bridge / Layer 2 SWITCH

A device that creates connection between two networks at layer 2 of the OSI model, which is the data link layer, is known as a bridge. Data frames are identified in the data link layer by a bridge (identical to packet data, however, it is usually known as frames in the data link layer). These data frames are stored for a short period of time in memory, after which the regenerated signal is forwarded as a new frame to another connected section of the network. Furthermore, it is also possible to denote data in TCP. As the bridge is able to store these frames, it can connect 10BASE-T and 100BASE-TX data links with entirely distinct transmission rates, without placing any limitations on the number of links.

FCS (CRC Cyclic Redundancy Check) refers to a bit in the data frame of a data link and is used to check the bit within the data frame. The purpose of this type of CRC is to determine if any damage has been caused to a data frame by the noise that often weakens the data signal in the transmission. It also verifies if the data has arrived at its correct destination. Data was damaged by Bridges Discard by examining the values in this field to stop it from being dispatched to other segments. Furthermore, network traffic (the number of datagrams transferred through the network) can be regulated by the bridge by self-learning technique of the address and the filtering function.

The address here refers to the Mac address, physical address, hardware address and adapter address, which is the particular address that is allocated to the NIC on the network.

When communication with host B is carried out by the host, just the data frame can be transmitted to host A. It is determined by the bridge if a frame should be forwarded on the basis of the address self-learning technique.

This is the part carried out by Layer 2 (data link layer) of the OSI reference model. This is why, bridges are frequently known as layer 2 switches (L2 switches).

There are a few bridges known as self-learning bridges that can identify if data packets should or should not be transferred to the adjoining segments. In this kind of bridge, the Mac address of all the frames it forwards is recalled by the bridge and is stored in its own memory table. This allows us to identify the network segment that includes devices that hold their respective MAC addresses.

A Bridge-enabled hub is known as a switching hub, while a repeater-only hub is known as a hub. A hub that is frequently employed in networks known as Ethernet is now called a Network bridge hub. A bridge-like function is offered by every port linked to the cable in the switching hub.

Router / Layer 3 Switch

A device that creates connection between two networks at layer 3 of the OSI model, the network level is known as a router that transmits data packets. The processing of the bridge occurs in compliance with the physical address (MAC address), whereas the router/Layer 3 switch is processed in accordance with the IP address. Therefore, the network layer address in TCP/IP turns into the IP address.

There can be a connection between a router and various data links. For instance, it can connect two Ethernet networks, or a single Ethernet to an FDDI. In the present times, the broadband router that is used by individuals to connect to the Internet at their homes or offices is also a type of router.

The network load is also shared by the router (as the router divides the data link, transmittal of the broadband message at the data link layer will not take place). There are certain network security properties in some routers. Hence, a very critical part is performed by the router in linking the network and the network equipment.

4 ~ 7 Layer Switch

Data is handled by Layer 4 ~ 7 from the transport layer to the application layer in the OSI model. When using the TCP/IP layer model, the sending and retrieval of data on the basis of the transport layer of TCP as well as the application layer over it is examined by Layer 4-7.

For instance, consider an enterprise-level Website that has high degree of concurrent traffic, a server or group of servers linked to the Internet as given in the URL. Currently, information content can be distinguished into game sites, resource downloaded sites and Websites. To fulfill the access requirements of the front-end, one server is not sufficient, which is why multiple servers are typically established. There is usually just one entry address for front-end access (the enterprise just opens a single access URL to the end user for user convenience). A load balancer may be included in the front end of these servers to divide the front-end access to multiple servers in the background using the same URL. The load balancer is part of the 4-7 layer switches (apart from load balancing through DNS). When multiple IP addresses are arranged using the same name, every customer that asks about the name is provided one of the addresses, which allows different clients to gain access to different servers. This method is also called the reuse DNS approach).

In practical communications, priority is given by

individuals to communication requests that need a greater degree of timelines, like voice calls. When there is a lot of congestion in the network, the processing of communication requests, like email or data forwarding, should be decreased in those situations were a minor delay would not cause any harm. This process is known as bandwidth control and is a significant function of layer 4 ~ 7 switches.

There are several applications of Layer 4 to 7. For example, special application access accelerators, WAN accelerators, and firewalls that prohibit illegal access on the Internet.

Gateway

A gateway represents a device in the OSI reference model that carries out the conversion and forwarding of data from the transport layer to the application layer (a router conventionally functions like a "gateway"). However, in this book, gateways are restricted to devices or elements in the OSI reference model that transform protocols at every layer over the transport layer). Similar to Layer 4 to 7 switches, data is processed at the transport layer and above; however, data is not only forwarded by the gateway, rather it is also converted. Typically, a presentation layer or application layer gateway is used. There is translation of two protocols that previously unable to communicate with one another directly.

A common example is the switching service between Internet mail and Mobile Mail. At times, Mobile mail may not be compatible with Internet mail due to the variations in "e-mail protocol" between the presentation layer and the application layer. The question that arises is why computers and phones that are connected to the Internet transfer e-mails among one another? A gateway is present between the Internet and the phone. It is the responsibility of the gateway to review different protocols, transforming them in a suitable manner one after the other and then sending the relevant data across. This enables computers and mobiles to transfer e-mails to one another, even when separate e-mail protocols are utilized.

Furthermore, when the www is being used (www), at times proxy server is required to regulate network traffic for security purposes. This proxy is a kind of gateway, and is referred to as an application gateway. The proxy server does not bring about direct communication with the client and server on the network layer. Rather, the transport layer regulates and processes the data and access to the application layer. A firewall refers to communication carried out across the gateway and is used in various applications to enhance security.

CHAPTER 4
ADVANCED NETWORKING

This chapter will enable us to obtain an extensive understanding of the reference models and the TCP protocol.

Physical Layer

The first thing that needs to be known about the "physical layer" of network configuration is its function. In comparison to other layers, the physical layer consists of a greater number of technologies and processes because of the kinds of transmission media, physical interfaces as well as their communication protocols. However, the key functions of the physical layer are quite simple, and include the following:

(1) Developing a Data Path:

"Data Path" signifies an entire data transmission channel. It may also be a segment of physical media or be connected with several physical media. There are three main stages in the overall data transfer, which include the activation of the physical connection, transfer of data and termination of the physical connection. A physical connection is established regardless of the number of physical media involved. To create an uninterrupted data transmission channel, the two data terminal equipment should be connected to each other.

(2) Transparent Transmission

Several kinds of transmission media exist in the physical layer (like various kinds of coaxial cable, twisted paid and optical fiber, etc.), each of which is supported by the respective communication protocols and standards. This shows that the various computer networks may have distinct "paths". Apart from repairing these distinct "paths", it is also ensured by the physical layer that these distinct "paths" are connected to generate paths that ultimately transfer the bit stream to the "physical layer" on the other end, the objective of which is to subsequently transmit it to the data link layer.

To ensure that these functions are accomplished, the physical layer should have the function of protecting various transmission media types and communication protocols. This would ensure that the parties communicating across the network are only able to observe that a "road" is available, irrespective of the particular "material" and the relevant standards utilized to construct these "roads". This demonstrates the "transparent transport" function of the physical layer.

(3) Transmission of Data

It is imperative for the final data to be transferred across the lowest "physical layer", regardless of the layer of the network configuration at which the communication is initiated as it is the only physical channel of the network communication. However, the bit is the transmission unit for the "physical layer" (where Binary 0 or 1 in the data denotes a bit). The fundamental objective of the "physical layer" is to transfer data in the order of bit stream to the receiver's physical layer across the physical layer interface and transmission medium.

(4) Data Coding

To allow for the transmission of data in an efficient and reliable manner on the "physical layer", it should be ensured that the data bit stream is able to move through the respective "channel". This includes the "physical layer" of data encoding functions as different kinds of data encoding are supported by the distinct transmission media (like non-zero-return code, zero-return Code, Manchester Code, differential Manchester Code, etc.).

(5) Data Transmission Management

There are certain functions of data transmission management in the "physical layer", like data transmission flow regulation, error management, activation and discharge of physical lines, and so on.

Datalink Layer

There is direct or indirect inclusion of the data link layer in computer network configurations (the functionality of the data link layer in the TCP/IP Protocol Architecture is part of the network access layer). The data link layer is almost the same as the physical layer beneath it, that is, they are used to construct a channel for communication and access of the network. It is just the physical layer that constructs a physical channel, while the data link layer constructs logical channels that are actually used for data transmission. Due to this, the TCP/IP Protocol Architecture that is extensively employed on the Internet, the data link layer and the physical layer are distributed into the network access layer.

The data link layer is situated in the lower layer of the "network layer" (known as the interconnect layer in the TCP/IP Protocol Architecture) of the network configuration. Therefore, one of its fundamental functions is to offer transparent and dependable data transfer services to the network layer (in a computer network configuration, the next layer serves the other one above it). "Transparent" suggests that the content, format or encoding of the data being transferred at the data link layer faces no limitations. This suggests that there are a few control characters that have distinct objectives (explained later in the chapter) and which can be transferred in the form of standard data so that they are not confused by the receiver as being control characters. When there is reliable transmission, it is ensured that there are no errors in the transfer of data from the sending end to the receiving end of the data link. On the whole, there are four major functions of the data link layer (the LLC sub layer in this case): transparent transmission, Data Link Management, encapsulation into frames and error management.

Network Layer

If the physical layer and the data link layer are contrasted with the intra-city traffic, comparison can be carried out between the network layers presented in this chapter and a transit station, dock or airport that creates connections within urban traffic. Similar to how passengers are transported from one location to another through a transit station, dock or airport, the network layer transmits data from one network to another or to a destination node within the network. It is not possible to have direct communication when the source and the destination are not present in the same network. A network layer is then required in this situation.

A very significant layer in network configuration is Network Layer (known as interconnect layer in TCP/IP Architecture), which is a complex layer in technology. It does not just resolve the issue of route and protocol identification, but also helps in decreasing network congestion by means of route selection strategy so as to enhance the reliability of network communication. The purpose of the network layer is to route packets from the source across the network path to the destination. This can be attained when the network layer is aware of the topology of the communication subnet and selects the appropriate path in the topology. The network layer should also make careful selection of the routing path to avoid coming across the situation in which certain communication lines and routers become overloaded, whereas others remain unoccupied.

The communication lines in the LAN are created by the physical layer and the data link layer put forward earlier, and these are comparable with the traffic lines in a city. The network layer explained in this chapter refers to the node that is used to link various local area network lines situated at the edge of the separate networks, and is similar to the edge of the city that provides connection to various urban transit points.

The network layer represents the third layer in the OSI reference model (equivalent to the second layer in the TCP/IP Protocol Architecture, the interconnect layer), and is situated between the transport layer and the data link layer. The major objective of the network layer is to accomplish transparent data transmission among the two network systems, such as routing, congestion control and Internet interconnection. The lowest layer of the end-to-end network communication (that occurs between the networks) is the network layer. It is the network layer's responsibility to form connection with the resource subnet over it (Osi/RM reference model transport layer and over four layers). In addition, this layer is the most complicated and important layer of the network communication-oriented lower three layers of the OSI/RM reference model.

The network layer is an outcome of the establishment of the computer network; however, it is not the outcome of a computer network. During the earlier times when the computer networks were established, a distinct local area network existed. We are aware of the fact that in the LAN, the physical layer and the data link layer create the communication link that may be used to provide communication access to the users. Hence, other layers like the network layer are not required. In addition, there was limited application of computer network at that time, and communication between the local area networks was not needed; hence, these local area networks did not require any connection between each other. However, as the computer networks developed and became widely known, it was noted that it was very important to create a connection between these separate local area networks one-by-one to develop a larger computer network. This would help in making the role of the computer networks more evident, allowing a greater number of people to make collective use of the server and hardware resources. This includes the interconnection of computer networks.

Then why is this network layer required? The answer to this is quite simple; as different networks have distinct network layer protocols and address specifications, if network communication protocols and address specifications of other networks cannot be recognized by users in a certain network, then data transfer between these networks is not possible. Consider the example of how the traffic rules and regulations of different cities are not the same. Every city is part of a distinct traffic police system, and does not permit traffic to move in and out of the city randomly. In a similar way, there are distinct design specifications of distinct networks, which are part of different organizations to be managed. In addition, they should be authorized and follow distinct protocols to allow communication between the networks.

A computer networks is typically a management boundary that is part of a particular company and managed by a given manager. Hence, while carrying out connection between computer networks, there are two things that should be taken into account at the same time: to authorize users to visit the networks of each other and share their resources, and to preserve the sovereignty of the management of every computer network. Therefore, it is not possible to solve an issue by just pulling off a cable (which does not resolve the issue of management independence). In various settings, two computer networks situated in distinct cities or even in different countries cannot be connected to each other through a tether.

Network layer is essentially involved in routing packets from the source node to the destination node. In majority of the computer networks, packet switching makes use of datagram packets to pass through multiple hops (the number of routers) to get to their destination.

Routing

Routing function refers to a packet switching path selection action, which is the fundamental function of the network layer. These functions can be compared with the way we select the best (not just the fastest, but a mix of both) route to transfer products.

A letter can be transported using various routes. Each route has a distinct approach of mailing, different length and time of mailing, and incurs a distinct amount of cost for transportation. The route should be selected after evaluating the total mailing cost, mailing time and the degree of reliability of the post office. Routing is identical to this process; it needs to take into account several factors, like channel bandwidth, line length, the cost of the port, line standard, etc. Different factors are considered by the different routing algorithms.

Routing is basically a means of transporting information from the source node to the destination node through the network. In simple terms, it indicates that packets from a single interface are transmitted to three layers of devices, and are aligned in accordance with the destination address of the packet, after which they are sent to another interface. However, there is at least a single intermediate node that needs to be faced in this routine route, which is the device that offer routing functions, like routers and layer 3 switches. The key distinction between routing and bridging is that bridging takes place at layer 2 (link layer) of OSI reference protocol, where distinct sections of the same network or sub network are connected, whereas routing takes place at Layer 3 (network layer) that is linked to a separate network or subnet.

The routing function can be attained based on the routing table within the router or three-layer switch. Routing is of two types: static routing and dynamic routing.

It is often required to configure static routing, particular within small lens, as it is quite simple to set up and manage. Static routing is appropriate for small networks that do not change often, like the local area networks. Nonetheless, a bigger WAN may have a more complicated topology and its network structure often undergoes changes; hence, static routing is not pertinent for this network, while dynamic routing shows greater flexibility and automation.

A significant feature of dynamic routing is that the routers that are part of a route in the network begin a dynamic routing protocol at the same time, after they have notified the networks to which they have a direct connection. Routing table entries will automatically be carried out by these routers, and each one does not have to be created manually by administrators. For bigger networks, this is the most convenient and easy routing alternative.

IP Addresses

IP protocol is the most significant protocol of Osi/Rm Network layer and the TCP/IP interconnect layer. This protocol is present in the transition period of IPV4 and IPv6. Therefore, the two versions of the IP address and relevant knowledge of the system is presented in this chapter.

In IPv4, 32-bit (4-byte) addresses are used; hence. there are 4294967296(232) within the overall address space for almost 4.3 billion addresses. Nonetheless, a few of these addresses are kept aside for exclusive objectives, like LAN private addresses (including almost 18 million addresses) and multicast addresses (around 27 million addresses). This is how it can be used directly in the wide area network, while there are even lesser number of public networks IP addresses routing.

A subnet mask can be understood by first comprehending the constitution of an IPv4 address. There are several small networks that constitute the Internet, and each of these has several hosts, which gives rise to a hierarchical structure. When developing the IPv4 address, every IP address is differentiated into two parts: a Network ID and host ID, which plays a role in facilitating the addressing function of IPV4 address. A question that is put forward is the number of bits that are network ID and host ID of an IPV4 address? If the number is not given, then there is no knowledge of the bits in the IPV4 address that denote the network ID and those that denote the host ID during addressing, which is achieved through a subnet mask presented here.

In the entire network architecture, communication subnet-oriented layers is the name given to the lowest three layers of OSI/RM seven-layer model, and it is the responsibility of these layers to create the communication channel. The transport layer and those above it are referred to as the resource-oriented subnet-oriented layers that carry out data communication among the Terminal Systems. The "transmission layer" and the subsequent three layers can also be differentiated into a communication-oriented layer that is typically responsible for the creation of communication channels and data transmission. The three layers, "session layer" , "presentation layer" and " application layer" are together referred to as application-oriented layers and do not have any data transfer function.

Application Layer

The topmost layer of the OSI/Rm and TCP/IP configurations is the application layer. Services are directly offered by this layer to users by making use of the services offered by the subsequent layers. It represents the interface that is present between a computer network and users. Similar to the services offered by other layers, there are particular communication protocols that help in fulfilling the service objectives of the application layer.

This layer is used on a routine basis by users, for example in web services, e-mail services, DNS (domain name service), file transfer service, DHCP (automatic IP address assignment service), remote login service, and so on. As the internet applications are developed and become popular, various new network application services emerge. In this chapter, a few of the most widely used services in TCP/IP network are presented.

The shared problems of TCP/IP network application in the application layer are solved by the application layer in TCP/IP, consisting of the supporting protocols and application services linked to network applications. Domain name service system (DNS), dynamic host configuration protocol (DHCP) and simple network management protocol (SNMP) is some of the supporting protocols. Some of the application services are E-mail service, web browsing service, remote login service, file transfer access service, etc. Furthermore, some protocols are linked to these standard network application services, such as Simple Mail Transfer Protocol, Hypertext Transfer Protocol, File Transfer Protocol, remote login (Telnet) and simple File Transfer Protocol.

The World Wide Web (www) service or web service is the most well-known and frequently employed application. HTTP (Hypertext Transfer Protocol) is the main application layer protocol for web services, and this can also be considered as the "hero behind the Hypertext Transfer Protocol" of Web services.

Background and History of TCP / IP

Currently, the most popular and extensively used protocol in a computer network is the TCP/IP Protocol. It is asked how the popularity of TCP/IP increased in such a short span of time. According to some, this is because TCP/IP is backed by PC operating systems like Windows and MAC OS. Though this is correct to some extent, it is not the main reason why TCP/IP has become so popular. The actual reason is that in the entire computer industry of that time, a widespread trend was created by the overall society to back TCP/IP so that different computer manufacturers adapt to this change and keep creating products to back TCP/IP. In the present times, there is hardly any system that does not back TCP/IP on the market.

Literally, TCP/IP may be considered to signify both TCP and IP protocols. In the practical sense, it often represents these two agreements. Nonetheless, most of the times, just the IP Communication should be collectively used in the group of protocols. Some of the TCP/IP protocols are IP or ICMP, TCP or UDP, TELNET or FTP, and HTTP. These are closely related to TCP/IP and form a vital part of the Internet. In general, TCP/IP represents these protocols; hence, TCP/IP is often known as the Internet Protocol Suite (the group of protocols constituting the Internet Protocol Suite).

The standardization procedure of TCP/IP Protocol is not the same as other standardization procedures, and they have two features" openness and practicality, which demonstrates if it is possible to use standardized protocols practically.

Openness is one of the features of TCP/IP Protocol that is elaborated by the IETF, which is an organization that permits anyone to take part in the discussion. People usually carry out routine discussions as e-mail conversations, and anyone can subscribe to these groups at any point they wish to.

Secondly, during the standardization process of the TCP/IP, significance is no longer given to the specification of a protocol on its own; however, the foremost task is to acknowledge that the technology can bring about communication. Hence, it is not surprising that a few people asserted that "TCP/IP only refers to first creating the program and then noting the specifications".

Though this is some form of exaggeration; TCP/IP does consider the practicality of executing a protocol when establishing a protocol specification (implementation: the creation of programs and hardware that allow a computing device to carry out particular actions or behaviors as anticipated by the protocol). Once the ultimate specifications for a protocol are applied, a few of these protocols are already present in a few devices and are able to communicate.

In this regard, when the general specification of a protocol are identified in TCP/IP, experiments may be carried out with people regarding performing communication between multiple devices that have used the protocol, and once something wrong is identified, they can be discussed further in the IEFT Modify protocols, programs or related documents in a suitable manner. The extensive discussions, studies and experiments ultimately give rise to a protocol specification. Hence, the practicality of the TCP/IP Protocol is quite high.

Nonetheless, the protocols that were not found to cause any problems because of the restrictions of the experimentation environment would be enhanced at a subsequent stage. The key reasons why OSI is not as widely used as TCP/IP is that it was unable to develop practical agreements in the earliest possible time frame put forward agreements to manage rapid technological innovation and execute late-stage improvement initiatives in a timely fashion.

The most extensively used protocol in a computer network is the TCP/IP. Hence, those who wish to create networks, manage networks and design and construct network devices, as well as carry out network device programming should essentially gain information about TCP/IP.

The hardware that is supposed to perform data transmission is present at the lower end of the TCP/IP. This hardware is the same as a physical layer device, like an Ethernet or a telephone line. No constant definition for it is available. This is because when varying transmission media (like the use of network lines or wireless) are used by individuals at the physical level, there will be different reliability, network bandwidth, delay, security, etc. In addition, there are no fixed indicators in these domains. In other words, TCP/IP Protocol has been put forward on the basis of the fact that interconnect devices are able to communicate with one another.

The network interface layer (often known as the network communication layer that integrates the network interface layer with the hardware layer) employs the data link layer in the Ethernet for communication purposes; therefore, it is part of the interface layer. This means that it should be considered as the "driver" that decreases the significance of NIC work prologue. Software that closes the gap between the operating system and the hardware is known as a driver. When the peripheral devices or extension cards are plugged directly in a computer or its expansion slot, they are not detected instantly and require the support of a relevant driver. A new NIC network card, for instance, require not just the hardware, but also the software to be used. Hence, drivers frequently need to be installed by people over the operating system so that they can use the additional hardware (There are several plug-and-play devices that work because drivers have already been built by the operating system of the computer over the network card).

The IP protocol is used by the Internet layer that is equal to layer 3 of the OSI model. Several IP packets are forwarded on the basis of the IP Address. Furthermore, IP functionality should be carried out by all hosts and routers linked to the Internet. TCP/IP functions are not essentially required to be carried out by other network devices connected to the Internet (like repeaters, bridges or hubs), rather they frequently need to have TCP/IP functions to supervise and handle repeaters, bridges, hubs, etc.).

IP refers to a protocol that transfers packets throughout a network, because of which data can be received across the Internet. Data can be sent through the IP Protocol to the other end of the world. The IP address is used here to function as the host identity (there should be a unique identification number of all of the devices that are linked to the IP network so that the particular device can be recognized. On the basis of the IP address, packet data is transmitted to the opposite end). The function of the Data Link Layer is also indicated by the IP address. The IP allows the hosts to perform communication with one another, irrespective of the data link beneath.

Though the IP is a packet switching protocol, a retransmission method is absent. Resending of packets does not take place even when the end host does not receive them. Hence, this kind of transport protocol is not reliable.

In case of an exception when moving the IP packet towards the destination address, which is not reachable, the sender is notified about the exception. For this purpose, ICMP is developed. At times, it is also used to determine the health of the network.

A protocol is needed to solve the physical address (MAC address) from the packet's IP address.

The transport layer is essentially responsible for ensuring that communication takes place between applications.

Numerous programs are simultaneously operating within a computer, which is why it is vital to determine the programs communication with each other. The port number is used to recognize these applications.

TCP refers to a connection-oriented transport layer that can make certain that communication between two communication hosts takes place. The transmission process can properly be handled by the TCP when there is loss of packets; transmission is not working properly and in other abnormal situations. Furthermore, bandwidth can successfully be used by TCP and relieve network congestion.

Nonetheless, to create and remove the connection, the packet has to be sent and received at least 7 times, which creates waste in network traffic. Furthermore, to increase the use of the network, different complex specifications are described by the TCP protocol that is not favorable for video conferencing (audio and video data set), in addition to other situations.

UDP is different from TCP in that it is a connectionless oriented transport layer. UDP is not concerned with whether the other end actually receives the transmitted data and whether it needs to find out if the other end has received the packet data, or if the other end has a connection with the network. Multimedia files frequently need to use UDP, like packet less data or multicast, broadcast communication and video communication.

Within the TCP/IP Layer, the functions of the session layer, application layer and the presentation layer within the OSI reference model are included in the application sequential implementation. Often, these functions are carried out using a single program or through multiple programs. Hence, when the application functions of the TCP/IP are closely examined, it can be seen that it executes not just the application layer of the OSI model, but also the session layer and the presentation layer.

The TCP/IP application architecture is mainly a part of the Client/Server Model. The server is the program that offers the service, while the client is the program to which the service is offered. In this communication method, there is pre-deployment of the service provider to the host, which is waiting to get requests that may be sent by the customer at any time.

A request can be sent by the client to the server at any point in time. At times, the server may deal with the exception and overload when the client is ready to wait for a while to issue a repeated request.

WWW (worldwide web) is a specification used to read data over the Internet and is also often known as Web, www, or W3. Users use a kind of browser known as the web browser (frequently called the browser in short). Some examples of browsers that are used quite extensively are Microsoft's Internet Explorer and Mozilla Foundation's Firefox. It is easy to surf the web using a mouse and a keyboard. This suggests that a single click of the mouse on a remote server is going to offer a variety of information to the browser. Text, images, animation and other types of information can be presented by the browser, which can also play audio and run programs.

HTTP (Hypertext Transfer Protocol) signifies the protocol used to carry out communication between the Browser and the server. The data is mainly transferred in the HTML (Hypertext Markup Language). In the www, HTTP is part of the OSI application layer protocol, whereas HTML is part of the presentation layer protocol.

E-mail refers to the use of Internet to send letters. An email can be shared between anyone with a connection, no matter how far they are from each other in the physical sense. E-mails are sent using the Protocol SMTP (Simple Mail Transfer Protocol).

People were only able to send e-mails in textual forward in the beginning (including just text messages; only 7-bit JIS encoded text could be sent by Japanese initially). However, MIME not describes the format of an e-mail message (a requirement for format of mail data that is extensively utilized over the Internet). It can also be utilized in www and web forums. Sounds, pictures and other kinds of information can also be sent now. It is also now possible to change the size and color of the message text (certain functions may not be shown completely because of the limitations of the mail-receiving software). The MIME explained here is part of Layer 6 of the OSI reference model, which is the presentation layer.

File Transfer (FTP)

When a file stored on another computer's hard drive is transferred to a local hard drive or from a local hard drive to another computer's hard drive is known as file transfer. FTP (File Transfer Protocol) is the protocol adopted in this process. The use of FTP has been prevalent for an extended time period (it was only recently that HTTP and WWW came into use for file transfer). One can select from the binary or text mode of the transfer (there is automatic change in line breaks for text-based file transfer between systems like Windows, MacOS or Unix; this also belongs to the presentation layer). When there is file transfer in FTP, two TCP connections are created; these include the control connections established to create transmission request and data connections used to perform the actual transfer of data (the control management of these two connections is the task of the session layer).

Remote Login (TELNET and SSH)

The ability to log on to a remote computer is known as the remote login, through which programs installed on that computer can run. The two most frequently used protocols for remote login across TCP/IP Networks are Teletext (the term used to represent Teletypewriter Network, also known as the default protocol) and SSH (short for secure shell). Various other protocols permit remote logins, like the R command for login in BSD UNIX systems and the x protocol in x window system.

Network Management (SNMP)

SNMP (Simple Network Management Protocol) is used for Network Management in TCP/IP. SNMP is used to managed bridges, routers, hosts, etc., and these are referred to as SNMP agents, while the segment that is managed is referred to as a Manager. The Manager and Agent here use the SNMP protocol.

Information regarding network interface, communication data, device temperature and abnormal data are stored in the agent side of the SNMP. The Management Information Base can be used to access this information, which is also called a network-permeable structural variable. Hence, during the network management of TCP/IP, SNMP is part of the Application Protocol, while MIB is part of the Presentation Layer Protocol.

When a network is bigger and more complicated, it

requires a greater degree of effective management. Administrators can use SNMP to assess network congestion in a timely manner, identify failures early on, and gather the information needed for network development in the future.

How are TCP / IP Transmitted over Medium?

In this section, the way data processing transfers from the application layer to the physical media when TCP/IP is used is discussed.

Packet Header

A header in every hierarchy is connected with the data being transmitted, which includes the information required for the layer, like the destination address to be dispatched and protocol-related information. The information offered for the protocol is generally the header of the package, while data is the content that is to be transferred.

There are two parts of the data packet transferred in the network, which include the first part used by the protocol and the other part in which data is transferred from the upper layer. The specification of the protocol presents a detailed description of the structure of the header. For instance, the domain that recognizes the upper layer protocol should commence with a given bit of the package, how checksum is calculated and the bit of the package that is to be added. There is no communication between two computers that recognize the serial number of the protocol and compute the checksum in different ways.

Hence, at the start of the packet, the way protocol should read the data is shown in a clear way. On the other hand, the information required for the protocol and how it can be processed will be understood by viewing the header. Hence, viewing the header of the package is the same as viewing the protocol's specification.

This is why people assert that the foremost one is similar to the face of protocol dispatching packets. Consider an example where an email is sent by A to B, with the message "Good Morning". In TCP/IP Communication, it signifies sending an e-mail from computer A to computer B. The process of TCP/IP communication can be described using this example.

Application Processing

The TCP/IP Communication commences when the application is launched to create a new message, after which the recipient's mailbox address is added, the content of the message as "good morning" is inserted using the keyboard and the "send" button is clicked. For instance, ISO-2022-JP or UTF-8 is used to encode

Japanese email and these codes are related to Osi's presentation layer functions.

Following code conversion, the actual message may not be dispatched immediate as some mail software is capable of sending multiple messages simultaneously. Users may also have the ability to press the "receive mail" button before they receive new mail. These kinds of administrative functions regarding when a communication connection should be established and when data is to be transmitted are, from a wider perspective, the tasks assigned to the OSI reference model at the session layer.

Data is sent by the application using the TCP connection, where the TCP connection is created at the point the message is sent. In this process, the application data is sent to the subsequent layer of TCP, after which the actual forwarding processing is carried out.

The Processing of TCP MODULE

It is the responsibility of TCP is establish connections, dispatch data and then disconnect, in accordance with the instructions of the application (that are equal to the session layer within the OSI reference model). Reliable data transmission is offered by TCP from the application layer to the opposite end.

To accomplish this function of TCP, a TCP header should

be connected to the front end of the application layer data. The TCP header consists of the source and destination port numbers (to determine the applications on the sending host and the receiving host), the serial number (data is the part of the packet that is to be sent), and the Checksum (Checksum) (to check that the data has been properly read) (to identify if the data is corrupted). The packet connected to the TCP header is then transmitted to the IP).

The Processing of IP Module

The TCP header and TCP data is taken by the IP from TCP like its own data, and its own IP header is then added to the front end of the TCP header. Therefore, the TCP header, and then the application header and the data come after the IP header within an IP packet. The receiver IP address and the sender IP address are included in the IP header. The information used to identify if the subsequent data is TCP or UDP comes right after the IP header.

Following the generation of the IP packet, the route or host that should accept the IP packet is determined by the reference routing control table. This IP packet is then transferred to the driver that has a connection with these routers or host network interfaces so that the data is actually transmitted. When the MAC address of the receiving end is not known, an ARP (Address Resolution Protocol) lookup can be used. When we are aware of the

MAC address of the other end, the MAC address and the IP address can be given to the Ethernet driver to accomplish data transmission.

Processing of Network Interface (Ethernet Driver)

The IP packet received from IP is simply data sent to the Ethernet driver. This data is linked to the Ethernet header and transmitted for processing. The Ethernet header consists of the receiver's MAC address, the sender's MAC address and the marked Ethernet type's MAC address. The physical layer is used to transfer the Ethernet packet created from the information given above to the receiving end. The hardware is used to compute the FCS (Frame Check Sequence) in the send processing, which is then included towards the end of the package. FCS aims to identify if noise has caused a packet to become corrupted or not.

Network Interface (Ethernet driver) Processing

After receiving the Ethernet packet from the host, the MAC address is obtained from the Ethernet packet header to identify if the packet has been sent to itself. The data is discarded if it is not sent to its own packet (there are several NIC products that prevent the data from being discarded, even if it has not been sent to its own packet. This is done to keep a check on network traffic).

If you receive a packet that has been sent to you, check

the type field in the header of the Ethernet packet to identify the kind of data that is being transferred by the Ethernet protocol. Here, the data type is clearly an IP packet, which is why it transmits the data to the processing IP subroutine, and if it is some other protocol, like Arp, it transfers the data to the ARP handler. To sum it up, if an unidentified protocol type is part of the type field at the head of the Ethernet packet, then the data is disregarded.

Processing of IP Module

The foremost and subsequent parts of the IP packet are received by the IP module, and the same kind of processing takes place. If it is determined that the IP address in the header is similar to your own IP address, it is possible for you to receive the data and check the protocol at the subsequent level. If TCP is the upper layer, TCP is provided the part following the header of the IP packet; while in the case of UDP, the part following the header of the IP packet is transmitted to UDP. With respect to the router, the address of the receiver is not their own address most of the times. This is when it becomes imperative to use the routine control table in the study, which should be transmitted to the host or router following data forwarding.

Processing of TCP Module

The CHECKSUM is first computed in the TCP module

to identify if the data is corrupted. It is then determined if serial number is used to receive the data. Lastly, the port number is checked to identify the particular application. After receiving the data, "an acknowledgement receipt" is sent by the receiver to the sender. If the sender does not receive the return message, the sender thinks that the data is not being received and so, it keeps sending the data repeatedly.

When complete data has been received, it is transferred to the application determined by the port number.

Application Processing

The data that has been sent directly by the sender is received by the receiver application. An analysis of the data shows the location of the recipient of the message, and the address is of host B. if there is no mailbox for host B, then an error message is sent back to the sender that says that this address is not available.

However, B's inbox is available for host B; hence, the email can be received by recipient B. The hard drive of the computer will store the message. Once the message is saved, a "process normal" receipt will be sent by the receiver to the sender. In contrast, if the message is not saved because the disk is full, a "handle exception" receipt is returned to the receiver.

Therefore, the mail client on host B can be used by user B to receive and review the email that user A has sent, stating "Good morning".

A service that is used for instant sharing and instant messaging between specified contacts in a circle is known as SNS (Social Network Service) or Social networking. It is possible to examine the process of sending or receiving SNS messages using a mobile terminal, just like the e-mail communication process. The communication carried out across mobile phones, smart phones and tablets involves packet data, and so the carrier specifies the IP address at the point they are installed with a battery and switched on. When an application on a mobile device is opened, connection with a given server is established and the information stored at the server is sent to the mobile terminal after the user has verified the username and password. The relevant content is then shown by the terminal.

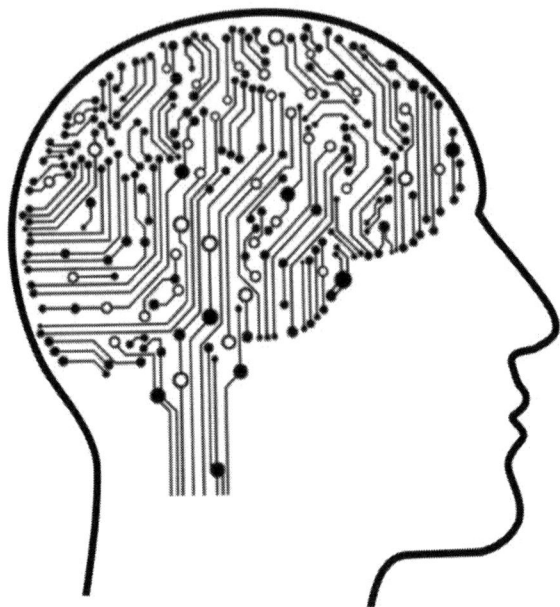

CHAPTER 5
MACHINE LEARNING &
COMPUTER NETWORKING

I t is essential to have a detailed understanding of Artificial Intelligence, machine learning, and deep learning prior to the discussion on how machine learning is applied in Computer networking.

Firstly, there is usually a misunderstanding among people regarding definitions. Artificial Intelligence is one aspect of computer science through which computers are enabled to work like humans. Machine learning is a part of Artificial Intelligence whereby computers are able to think like humans due to detailed data being provided. Complex algorithms are utilized for images, text, and face recognition through Deep learning, which is a part of Machine learning.

There are interconnections between all the three technologies, which enables better performance of computer networks and also function as an intrusion detection system. Following is a concise discussion on Artificial Intelligence, Machine learning, and Deep learning.

When computers were introduced in the 1950s and 1960s, Artificial Intelligence was also being worked on in University labs. The first set of researchers emerged due to the Turing test suggested by Alan Turing, and included expert systems, knowledge-based system, the mathematical proof system, in addition to landmark technology and implementation of artificial intelligence.

However, during that time, there was not adequate facility for further development of Artificial Intelligence, either due to computing speed of computers or its associated programming and algorithm theory. Similar to Exploring Wild China, there are two entirely different things to go to a new continent and truly making it prosper. Just like that, for instance, in 1951, a paper version of a chess program was published by Alan Turing, who is one of the innovators of Artificial Intelligence and Computer Science. However, these complex calculations could not be performed on computers at that time. Due to this reason, in the 1960s, the interest of general public and the researchers diminished with regard to Artificial Intelligence

I developed the speaker-independent continuous speech recognition between 1980s to the 1990s at the Carnegie Mellon University. This system was implemented on Apple Computer Systems which is considered the golden period for researchers of AI and product developers. Use of traditional semiotic-based methods is not used anymore by me and other researchers. Instead, further developments are being made in statistical-model-based methods in areas such as machine translation and speech recognition. In some applications, for example pattern recognition, artificial neural networks are also being applied. The deep blue computer was a big success over the Human Gary Kasprov in 1997.

However, in that era, the technological achievements were not adequate enough to surpass the psychological expectations that intelligent machines required. For instance, with regard to speech recognition technology, although the statistical model was a big achievement, it was not good enough to be accepted by the average person. The speech recognition App that I developed at Apple was mainly applied for promotions and presentations, having little practical significance. All in all, even though Artificial Intelligence is backed by extensive scientific experiments and researchers, and even developed interest of people, it was not entirely successful and is yet not aligned well with business models and requirements of the public.

Beginning from 2006 to 2010, computing speeds drastically improved with the development of deep learning techniques. Thus, with the immense data collected in the Internet Age, a new path of recovery was paved for Artificial Intelligence.

When something new is presented, people usually have a psychological limit to accept it, similar to their reaction to any external stimulus. The level of intensity of external stimuli like light, sound and electricity is not much for people to react on it. However, reaction occurs when the external stimuli is more than the least stimuli that an individual is able to perceive. There are specific absolute feelings of people like "seeing things" and "hearing voices". This minimum level of stimulus, which is psychologically considered an absolute threshold, is what causes a person to observe and react.

Same is the situation with Artificial Intelligence. Considering image recognition, in the initial days of artificial intelligence when a computer would identify a face in a given picture, it was usually around 50% correct as an average person would consider it as a toy and not intelligent. With progress in technology, the accuracy of face recognition algorithms improved to around 80-90%. It was not an easy task for researchers; however, average people are still not able to accept the results. Reason being that out of five faces, one is wrongly identified, which is not acceptable. It could be agreed that the program works well, yet it cannot be accurate enough to replace what a human eye can do. Human security will be replaced by computer security systems for identification tasks only when precision of the computer's face recognition is almost the same or even better than that of humans. This means the main concern is that face recognition applications could be close to or even a level higher than that of average people.

Thus, when it is stated that "AI is here", it signifies that real problems could be solved through deep learning or Artificial Intelligence. Artificial Intelligence has constantly exceeded the psychological level of acceptance when it comes to Machine Vision, automatic driving, data mining, speech recognition, and other applications. It is for the first time that it would be utilized to create actual value.

How Does Computer Learn?

What are the laws that computers develop? This is dependent on the type of machine learning algorithm being applied.

Consider an algorithm similar to a child learning to read an idea. It is observed by teachers and parents that when children start learning how to read, we differentiate "one", "two" and "three" by telling them that a stroke is one, two strokes is two characters and that three strokes is three characters. Understanding and implementing this is easy. But this rule might not be applicable when new characters are to be learnt. For instance the mouth would also be three strokes yet it is not exactly three strokes. Generally we teach the children that the mouth is the box and row is the three. This pattern keeps increasing however the number of words is still increasing. Following this, the children understand that a "field" is a box, but again it is not mouth. In this case, we teach the children that "field" is the box which has a "ten". Then we can tell children that "field" below the head is "a", above the head is "by" while above and below is "Ten". There are many children who understand through this step-by-step study of the characteristics of the law through correct guidance. They understand summary of the law, remember new Chinese characters, and even learn numerous Chinese characters.

Deep Learning

One method of machine learning is Deep Learning. It has flexibility in its expressiveness and enables experimentation by the computer till the required result is achieved. It seems that it is not quite different from other traditional approaches of machine learning that were mentioned previously. However, its purpose is to differentiate, as per characteristics, various classes of objects present in a high dimensional area. The expressive power in traditional machine learning and deep learning are extremely different.

Simply put, the process involved in Deep learning is that it utilizes the data a computer is attempting to learn and places that data in a complex and multilevel data process network, also known as deep neural network. Following this, it is checked as to whether the network's resulting data that was processed meets the given requirements. If requirements are met, the network is used as a target model. If requirements are not met, the network parameters are adjusted constantly till the requirements are met.

Consider that the data which needs processing through deep learning are the "flow" of information and a massive network of pipes and valves is the deep learning network. The entrance and exit of the network is a quantity of pipe openings. There are several layers of the water network, with each layer having valves for flow control and for regulating the water flow direction. There can be various combinations of total layers and the quantity of regulating valves as per the needs of various tasks. There could be even more than thousand regulator valves for complex tasks. Each control valve in every layer, in a water pipe network, is linked with the entire number of control valves in the subsequent layer via a water pipe. This results in formation of a front-to-back completely interlinked layer by layer system. This is an example which shows that installation and connection of pipes vary according to the type of deep learning models.

Side note: Deep learning can be observed on a bigger scale through the presently available visualization tools. One example is Tensor Flow which is Google's well-known deep learning framework. It runs a web version of a device which present real-time aspects of the overall web as the deep learning tasks through easy diagrams are performed.

Lastly, one significant aspect is that mathematical formulas and arguments are purposely excluded in the above mentioned deep learning approach. The popularization of deep learning with water networks is an approach which was only applicable for the general public. This is an inaccurate and incomplete picture for computer science and math professionals. The flow control valve correlation with the weight adjusted linked with every neuron in a deep neural network is not mathematically equivalent. In the entire depiction of the water pipe network, the gradient descent, cost function, back propagation, and other significant aspects of deep learning algorithm are not included. The question thus is that whether professionals should begin a new professional tutorial or should they understand deep learning.

We can now review a few examples of the way machine learning algorithm may be applied to computer networking.

The field of computer networking is quite bizarre, and frequently faces threats from hackers and scammers who try to convert this valuable field into an unpleasant one by plaguing it with viruses, Trojans, ransoms, and other dangerous stuff that cause a significant damage to the networks in terms of time, energy and money.

K-Nearest Algorithm

It is a well-known machine learning algorithm that may be used to identify network shells and span content within the network.

Decision Tree Algorithm

This algorithm can be used to identify irregular functions in the network using the large amount of sample data it has gathered.

Random Forest Algorithm

The random forest machine learning algorithm is capable of identifying irregular functions within the network and also brute force attacks through FTP.

Naïve Bayes Algorithm

Network shells and DDOS attacks within a computer network can be identified using Naïve Bayes algorithm.

Logistic Regression Algorithm

Logistic regression algorithms can be used to prevent java overflow attacks that are frequently made by malicious hackers.

Support Vector Machine

Support Vector Machine is known for its ability to identify Botnets as well as XSS vulnerability in web-based applications.

K-Means and DB-Scan Algorithm

These algorithms can be used to identify different kinds of attacks that are made on computers with a high degree of precision.

In addition, there are other deep learning algorithms that may help you in monitoring your employees at all times to ensure they do not make any errors. The security of networks can be enhanced significantly by using machine learning and deep learning techniques in computer networks. There is a lot of potential of machine learning with computer networks for the future.

CONCLUSION

I would like to thank you for going through the entire book Computer Networking for Beginners: The Complete Basic Guide to Master Network Security, Computer Architecture, Internet, Wireless Technology, and Communications Systems. I hope that it was enlightening to you and assisted you in acquiring the tools you needed to accomplish your objectives.

You should now move on to acquire more information about computer networking from different advanced textbooks. To examine computer networks in more detail, try to observe the different hardware you come across in your daily life.

As a follow up to this module, do go over the introduction to machine learning and artificial intelligence that we have provided as it will help you in enhancing your skills in the field.

To give you a short overview of the material covered in this e-book. We presented the definitions, history and fundamentals of networking by presenting a thorough overview of a network and several examples. A detailed discussion on network protocols was then provided. Finally, a discussion on Artificial Intelligence and machine learning was carried out in terms of Computer

Networking.

I would just like to say in the end that if this book helped you in any way, I will really appreciate a review on Amazon!